THE TRAUMA OF AN
AMERICAN EDUCATION

Sixty Years of Stories

Peace

Teague Skye.

T E A G U E   S K Y E

Charleston, SC
www.PalmettoPublishing.com

The Trauma of an American Education
Copyright © 2022 by Teague Skye

Paperback ISBN: 978-1-68515-782-1
eBook ISBN: 978-1-68515-783-8

DEDICATION:

This entire work is dedicated to our beloved Claylady, Michelle Rhodes, and Spirit Brother, James Luckner, who are the only humans we have known who have never walked away from us, never pushed us aside, never clung to us with demands of their own, never judged or criticized us for being who we are intrinsically, never demanded we be anything other than true to ourselves. They saw us, still see us, and care unconditionally in a world fraught with puppet strings of expectation everywhere. Without their undying, unwavering, consistent support, we would not only not have completed this work, we would not be here on the planet to do so. There is no doubt. May you each and all discover your own Claylady and Spirit Brother and may they be as true to you as ours have been to us.

Much gratitude to all the folks with whom we have worked in any capacity. Thank you for your faith, trust, and patience; for your willingness to throw caution to the wind and accept responsibility for yourself and your own learning; for your sense of humor in the darkest of times, your kindness in the most difficult, and for adding your efforts and your voice to the outliers of society who would be in the center leading if we had a culture rather than merely a society. Thank you all for allowing us to walk along on a bit of your journey toward becoming yourselves; thank you for teaching us lessons we would never have learned your guidance."

May we all heal and thrive. Peace y'all.

TEAGUE SKYE, c1989, WITH THE STUDENTS WHO POURED THE NEW FOUNDATION PLACING THEIR HANDPRINTS IN THE CEMENT.

AUTHOR'S NOTE:

This book is comprised of my own recollections and as such represents one minuscule perspective; I am certain there are myriad others out there regarding the same events as many were involved. Therefore, if you read this and have another viewpoint to share, please feel free to write and publish your own book. I'd buy one. Also, if you think you recognize yourself in here you are most likely incorrect. I have changed names, genders, even at times localities, and I have used no real names nor locations as originally named. So there. Besides, if ya wanna sue me, all yer gonna get is a 2007 corolla. May real learning occur everywhere and may schools as we have known them dissolve away like sugar cubes in warm pee so something far more real and meaningful and courageous can occur in this country. Peace y'all.

MY EDUCATION.

My first formal educational experiences began a couple of months before I turned five when I walked to kindergarten alone. Although most of my many brothers and sisters also walked to school at the same time each morning, the kindergarten was in a school different than any they needed to walk to, and so I walked alone. Had I only tasted ease in life until then it would certainly qualify as my first serious trauma. As it was, it was just another and further proof that the grown-ups were not only lost and clueless but dangerous and terrifying. After that, it was more of a roller coaster through hell than a merry go round, which is what it generally can amount to for most folks.

> *"Children must be taught
> how to think,
> not what to think."*
> *- Margaret Mead*

Kindergarten was a warning shot. Sadly, it was a formative one which left me feeling as though I had a cannon ball sized void between my ribs where my upper guts should have been. Instead of guts, there was an empty hole, a clean shot, see-through, like a Saturday morning Elmer Fudd cartoon or something but with a soundtrack more appropriate to the film **Rosemary's Baby**. This was certainly an entryway into a level of Hades not described in **Dante's Inferno**, which I was somewhat familiar with due to having been read many selections from the Encyclopedia Britannica collection by my sister mum that previous summer and having enjoyed some of William Blake's prints as a result. Despite being one of the youngest in the class age-wise, I was much older than many of my classmates. Decades older.

In 1964, childhood trauma had yet to be "discovered". No one spoke of abuse unless it was a neighbor mistreating a yard dawg too viciously and too openly. What happened at home, stayed there; decades before the Vegas saying. In the back of the closets and the basement corners and moldy crud collecting in the cracks everywhere, it hung and rotted. And, of course, teachers had a full range of negative responses to unacceptable behavior, or merely to their own symptomatic frustration with too many children in too small a space for far too long a period of time each day. It even had a name - corporal punishment - and it was still legal in every state. Adults could do whatever they wanted to "their" children or students; the cruelty of ageism is not unknown to children. Anything went. So I got to be abused there as well. Harassed and hated.

I still wear scars on my hands from the teachers who walked about with a ruler extending from their right sleeve as though an extra appendage fit for cruelty. I had a thing for touching to understand. We currently refer to this as "tactile learning", a term coined by John Gardiner in the 1980s with his "discovery" of various types of intelligence other than the mere academic aspect educators had been convinced mattered until then. But not then; not in 1964. Then it was unnecessary, snooping, even rebellious! Rebellious? At age four and five? And let's all remember that when we are four and five years old, we key off of "grown-ups" enough to force ourselves to become what they say we are. Not even if they are cruel, but **especially** if they are cruel, for then a child's very life and sanity may depend on becoming exactly what they name her, what they demand he become. At home, my middle name was "trouble"; I knew this as I had heard it enough in my short five years on the planet in a household wherein chaos was only ever disrupted by rage. And believe me, by the time I had gotten out of that particular hellhole of a school, I was well into my fifth year and supposedly causing a great deal of "trouble" everywhere I went.

I have no clue what the kindergarten teachers' names were. I have little recollection of any of it other than that we were expected to have a morning nap on these little rag woven throw rugs and I hadn't seen a nap in years regardless of the time of day. I remember there were two women called teachers, and that neither were happy about me being there, for I asked questions. I remember this was not okay, to ask questions in school. I was smart; I learned quickly and thoroughly and soon kept my questions to myself or for my sister mum to hopefully answer later. I remember that despite refusing to weep in front of anyone, despite refusing to cry even when a broken clavicle was sticking through my shoulder and worse, I wept as I walked there and back daily, quietly, and alone, ensuring there was no sign of any such "weakness" by the time I returned to the house I lived in with too many people where it was my responsibility to care for the baby, only a few months old, every afternoon.

We never referred to it as "home". It was the house, or the parent's house, the "p's" place or house, and later, it became hell house. The neighbors began to call it that, inspired by the screaming that made its way from wherever the nasty fight was going down inside, at any and all hours but primarily after dark, out into the neighborhood.

I remember much more about first grade. I got to walk to school with two of my older siblings and my teacher was a living saint. A first-year teacher still operating under the assumption that we were all precious and valued by the larger society, she was lovely, but incorrect. Still, it was a great break. For those months of first grade, I had a place to go during the day which was as safe a place as I had ever found, for she tolerated no meanness; I never recall her attacking me for my lack of manners or uncivilized behavior. She discovered early on that I could read, and she actually brought me books to keep me busy while everyone else practiced with Jane and Spot and Puff, who I was surprised to discover, was not, after all, a dragon. However, I'm afraid it set me up for a serious disappointment the following year, and increasingly every year thereafter.

My second-grade teacher had the unfortunate circumstance of having a husband MIA in Vietnam; halfway through the school year he was reported as a POW, then deceased. She was not kind. Her response was not simply to despise all of her charges, but to line us all up and beat us on a daily basis. At least once. She went through quite a few pointers that year as I recall, which was her weapon of choice. Yardsticks were okay; they certainly beat out rulers merely due to physics – the longer stick afforded a longer wind up swing. But yardsticks had little girth, and therefore broke when they wanted to really wail on a kid's ass end. So she used a pointer, a rounded pole as long as a yardstick with, as the name indicates, a point on the end, sometimes rubberized and other times metal. No one went home and said they got beat at school, unless for some sick reason they wanted to get beat again, for the teacher was still always right and no one I had met believed in sparing the rod, ever.

I have few memories of third and fourth grade, perhaps because I went to school less and less. Things were getting more interesting and dangerous at the house, and I often cut school to stay home and try to protect the mum.

In addition, I was already a marked kid by both teachers and students given my rather odd ways. When the third-grade teacher caught me surreptitiously sneaking bits of paper into my mouth to eat in an effort to calm my constant nausea, she announced to the entire class that I was "disgusting" and suggested they help me satisfy my hunger by showering me at every chance with little bits of paper. Or balled up wads. The students were happy to comply with the teacher's wishes; they'd already been actively despising me for three years by then and were well practiced. They showered me at every literal turn in the day, and even piled little paper balls in my desk with notes urging me to "fill up" or "eat me" whenever I was away from it. Fun, developmentally-sound situations such as this marked my third-grade year. The only other distinct memory I have is that of the teacher's poorly applied blood red lipstick which caught at her front buck tooth. She evidently applied it consistently throughout the day and would have been considered a marked woman by the students had she not wisely diverted their attention toward me. In all fairness to her, I was an easy mark and had been for years. By now, it was simply a role I played wherever I went.

In fourth grade I got my own rather new permanent front teeth broken by a friend of my older brother who thought it was hilarious. It was not. After I returned from the dentist who I am certain worked at Auschwitz or something, I had shiny silver caps on my front teeth, and the teacher, surprised to see me at the doorway, grabbed my arm and immediately marched me up to stand in front of the class to show what stupidity looked like. I do believe she needed a mirror. But it all mattered less and less. I wasn't going to last there much longer anyway.

By the end of fourth grade, I'd told the principal off so they had a social worker in to see me. It was my first of what became a lifetime of betrayals by social workers, therapists, counselors, and psychiatrists. I obviously have a vivid memory of the event. I can, 54 years later, describe the room and the woman sitting across from me in detail. I can see the way the sun rays moved slowly across the table, making the tiny faces appearing to me in the wood grain shimmer and wink. Miss Hill, after speaking at me for a bit, told me something which surprised even me, something I have never forgotten. She told me I smiled too much, suggesting that it made the teachers nervous and that I may wanna curb all that smiling. Now I was really confused. I mean, I never claimed to understand any of the mess they called school, but smiling? Smiling was now a bad thing? Jesus tits.

Now I'm gonna stop and explain something here, something I had learned long before I ever even knew about this layer of hell called school. I spent a bit of time in hospital as an infant and toddler which in those days meant a room full of cribs and babies screaming. It also meant no visitors since it was far from the house in northern Michigan where I was born and my family was living, and being sixth of eight children, or "characters" as my father would always clarify for others, I wasn't exactly a priority for my folk's time and energy. Still tiny, but old enough to pull myself up to a vertical position using the crib bars, I noticed that the nurses actually detoured around the children who cried, but when we smiled, they liked us better and therefore paid us more attention. This is my first vivid memory. The room, the wailing, me watching while standing in my crib. Me noticing. Me donning a smile and hoping. It ends there. I was simply acclimating to what I believed was the world. This was then supported later by the fact that when I was very ill, or injured, as was increasingly the case, I was praised mightily for not ever complaining, for taking whatever the pain of the day was without argument or fuss, for being what my old man called "a good little soldier". It was the only praise I received from him and it mattered mightily. Evidently, teachers were even more nervous about children than nurses and parents were. I do believe however that it was at this exact point that I decided somewhere deep within myself that I was no, not ever going to fit in, and so I may as well accept it, suck it up, and go it alone. I was ten years old at the time. Ten years old people.

I was ultimately, in fact, expelled shortly thereafter. I had been attacked one too many times by the principal. I turned on her, told her to fuck off, screaming that my older brother would use her to wipe up the halls. I no longer smiled. I was a quick learner. I had to switch schools, and I did, but I never really went again. Not with any consistency. Besides, one of the two teachers whose rooms I had been relegated to at the new school had a penchant for grabbing me by the front of my shirt, hoisting me off the ground a few feet, and slamming my body and head against the lockers. I suppose he was trying to get my attention. It didn't work. By the time I got to what was supposed to be the sixth grade, I wasn't anywhere near my body. That had proved far too dangerous in the past couple of years; I was already fairly dissociative, particularly should things get too interesting or painful. In the teacher's defense, I don't think I would have wanted to tolerate the likes of me at ages 11 and 12. I believe my once rather astounding vocabulary had melded into a two-word phrase; when I bothered to speak at all, "fuck off" seemed to say it all for me by then.

There was a single person with whom I became dear friends somewhere in fifth grade and with whom I did speak- my dear, dear pal and first love, Jess. Jess was suffering, dying actually, from leukemia cancer. She had no hair and was constantly bullied because of it. I had filthy hair and smelled of piss and was bullied for it. Small animals can be ruthless to those who are different, (google the pink monkey experiment sometime and you'll see exactly what I mean), and humans are most obviously small animals in our younger ages. Jess had no friends but me, and I had no friends but her. Of course, being small animals there was no room for rights or sensitivities to deeper relevancies such as friendship, and what that could really mean to someone alone in the world, or in constant danger in the one place that was supposed to be safe. So when Jess went into the hospital for the last time, I wasn't ever told. I was never invited to say good-bye for I was only 11, and you had to be 12 or over to visit someone in hospital back then. Besides, who would have let me know anyway? No one had any interest in me unless I was making a mess bleeding all over the place or if I hadn"t completed chores properly. My best and dearest and only friend died and the only way I knew was that after she didn't show up to school for months, I warily asked the only person I trusted minimally in the entire place to find out for me what had happened, the elementary school librarian. She had already been told. She did that adult wincing grimace thing they do and apologized as though for all adults everywhere and their unfeeling transgressions against children.

"Oh honey," she came around the desk and scrunched down to my level. "I'm so, so sorry no one thought to let you know." She reached out for my hands with hers; I took a step back and put my hands behind my back.

"She's dead, isn't she?" I demanded, squinting at the carpet angrily.

She looked down at the swirls in the carpet as though divining a response. It evidently proposed simplicity.

"Yes, yes. She passed in February," she almost whispered.

I narrowed my eyes further and looked out the window at the ever-present gloom of south Pittsburgh.

"Well," I said, still staring at the murky gray now streaming down the windows, "Just goes to show."

She was quiet, looked perplexed, then had to ask.

"Shows what honey?" I wondered if she even knew my name.

I looked down, shook my head no, and walked away. I wish I had thanked her.

I guarantee you that no one knew exactly why I was "acting out". Oh, they made their usual, then "extra special", effort to do what they had to do in such cases. I had been inherited as a "behavior problem" from another school, so it was deemed necessary evidently for me to see some strange guy about once a month or so whom I was supposed to trust enough to tell all of my secrets. I was often missing in action so perhaps he tried to see me more. Anyway, I was supposed to talk to this guy but I wasn't a complete idiot. I knew exactly who held the power and my life in their hands and it wasn't anyone that had anything to do with this or any other school. These were not people to be trusted. No one was to be trusted. No one. If they thought I was gonna spill anything, they were more thorough idiots than even **I** had suspected. In retrospect, given that by then it was well known throughout more than the neighborhood thanks to the newspapers that one of my older brothers was a known and rather expansive drug dealer in the area, perhaps they were actually trying to get some sort of information from me. I have no idea, but I know what they got was what everyone else got at that point. "Fuck off," in varying tones and intensities.

Back in the day, elementary school usually went from Kindergarten through sixth grade; junior high followed and I suppose from what little I know of the whole ordeal, it was intended as a sort of juniorized high school experience.

It was then students moved from a full day with a single known torturer to several unknown torturers a day; this meant bells ringing and classes changing and believe me, all manner of nasty nonsense went down in those hallways. At a moment's notice someone could decide to throw a punch or throw someone considered lesser into a corner to warn or feel up. On the other hand, junior high also offered a taste of classes unrelated to anything academic and the freedom to sit outside at lunch. However, most of my experience with junior high comes from a limited time spent actually there, in the building, physically or otherwise.

Whenever I did go into the school building for some strange reason, I was usually rewarded by further confirmation of how lost we were as a society and as individuals. There was absolutely nothing at the place that ever fed me in any positive way other than one art class which only lasted a few weeks. I do not think I am alone in this. There is no need to work to imagine this if you're a product of the American public education system; you can probably recall a single incident within the junior high or middle school scene clearly and with a leaden stomach. I have no idea what leads any educator to believe it is a good thing to shove about a thousand people suffering through the first throes of adolescence into a closed building wherein there is absolutely no attention paid to this fact, other than perhaps in a health class. Though I wouldn't really know, to tell the truth, as I never attended a health class. Indeed, I was so infrequently in attendance and so frequently a "problem" when I did show up that by the end of seventh grade, when I somehow managed to make it to home room, another pre high school warm up, I was simply told that the principal needed to see me, given a note, and excused immediately. No one wanted me in their classroom for any period of time. Mind, seventh grade was merely the first of a three-year sentence.

I do believe at this point I had been reduced to only two behavioral scenarios in public. One was complete shut down and the other was absolute manic mayhem. On shut down, I could have been confused with a patient stuck inside depressive catatonia. I simply checked out as my dissociative skills at this point were polished enough to be sorcerer like. One moment I was there in the principal's office, sitting in front of the huge polished desk w framed diplomas behind him, the next, I was nowhere; I didn't even exist. I was frequently in the chair due to a manic mayhem scenario, which simply meant that somewhere along the line, in a classroom or a hallway, I had somehow created absolute mayhem, reverting to it as the only outlet for an anger and frustration so deep that there was no longer solid ground beneath my feet. I lashed out at times in a blind frantic attempt to find something solid to hold fast to; the world could all slip into a terrifying place of monsters vying for my flesh at a moment's notice. And of course, my regimen of way too much weed and acid wasn't necessarily helpful at that point.

Chaos can be achieved readily in a junior high school wherein everyone is suffering from raging hormones and boundary issues. It requires as little as any attack requires in such a place; scream out some nonsense in a class, throw a book or a pen, attack a set of lockers with a shoe, start singing something crass loudly, simply refuse to do whatever is demanded with a steely stare. Honestly, if I as a teacher ever met me as a student in a public school classroom, I would have met my match. What I did not ever do however, was attack another student; I never started a fight or teased or bullied, ever, for I knew what that felt like and decided long ago I had no interest in modeling the torturers and rapists I had no option but to contend with. In retrospect, I see that I must have not seen the teachers and administrators, so often "trying to help" me out, as human beings with feelings, for I did lash out at them, without any consideration for their welfare, or mine. I had long ago lost any semblance of self preservation. I was in self destruction mode 24-7.

And yes, I have to wonder about that. Did I really view adults as inhuman? Why would I not? Everyone who had ever been "in charge" of me had been either cruel or missing in action. Or both. The only thing I could ever depend on was having to contend with the adults' ridiculous or dangerous or mean demands as well as the fact that at any moment, without warning and for no foreseeable reason, they could go batshit crazy and do some pretty vicious crap. That's what I knew about adults; that's the sum total of what I had experienced.

As it was, I spent most of my junior high years, when I deigned to enter the building, in the principal's office, ignored, in a desk in the corner facing the wall. Speaking wasn't allowed, nor was eating or sleeping. I doodled, all over the worksheets I had been handed as though a facet of my sentence for crimes I often had no realization I'd committed.

Now and then I'd sneak a piece of broken glass or an old safety pin out of my backpack or pocket, quietly roll my sleeves up, and check to see if I was still alive. If there was no blood, perhaps I could finally rest. No one ever noticed. No one ever looked at me, and I certainly never mentioned it. This was long, long before there was any awareness regarding "cutters". It was all just a bad dream, a nightmare, this thing some called life. Who did they think they were fooling? Everyone else I guess, as I was the only one there, in what the office staff referred to as "your desk". It was the only property I identified with in the entire place. The only spot in which I felt I belonged. My desk. My spot. My death.

Everyone I hung with who attended junior high school back then would meet out behind the school gym in the mornings and at the end of the school day in what we little hippies referred to as our "smoking area", though much more than smoking went down there. This was where we had a smoke before school, but also where we met up to buy and sell weed, coke, speed, reds, blotter acid, and other specialty items. This was where we decided to party for the day, or where we figured out where the high school kids were partying so we could join them. It was where we failed to wake up; where we joined up with other posturing, lost souls so that we could make our way in circles spiraling downward as a pack I suppose.

It must have been eighth grade that I turned 13. The day I turned 13, i went back to the house in late afternoon to make some dinner for whomever was there and would want to eat. I still had a couple of siblings and a mum to consider, though less and less. My little sister had found her way to a neighbor's house where there were a couple of kids her age to play with and a mum who cooked dinner every night without fail; the one brother still living there was more than able to watch his own back. Or so I thought. The mum had found her way out of her bedroom sanctuary and was starting to realize she didn't have to take whatever shit was shoveled her way. Unfortunately, she often chose me as the person to whom to shovel it over to. She had yet to develop the courage to send it back from whence it came. I walked into the house the afternoon I turned 13 and the fury that had been building in the poor woman had evidently overflowed way, way beyond capacity. And there I was, easy target, bingo.

"Where have you been?" She screamed into my face at very close range while smacking me and slamming my shoulders and head around pretty good.

Now remember, I'd been tripping fairly regularly for years so it wasn't as though I had any wits left to gather before I tried to respond. And the fact is, she would have taken me completely by surprise regardless of my state of mind. Who was this woman and why was she attacking me? I was totally lost. Still, I did what I always did when being beaten, put the body into a fetal position while still standing and evacuated all consciousness. Standard procedure; keep all the most fragile body parts as covered as possible and get out as soon as possible in any way possible. First mentally, then physically.

"The school called again!" She was bellowing and screaming over and over. "Where have you been? You haven't been to school in weeks! Where the hell have you been?"

I remained silent, waiting for the next blow, finding and maintaining a stance ready to bolt. "They're going to fine us!" she continued. "Who's going to pay for that? They'll put you in juvenile hall! Is that what you want?"

And then, the two statements I took completely to heart, having still not protected mine enough I guess. The two statements that I held close to remind myself as many minutes of as many days as possible for years afterward that I was a total worthless shit and deserved nothing. It became my creed. I am nothing. I am no one. I am not.

"You're just like him," she backed off and spit the words at me slowly, one by bitter one. We both knew who she meant. And no, it wasn't my rage-infested old man. It was far worse than that. It wasn't the first time she had made the reference, but it was the most violent.

I will stop here and tell you that should you ever be angry as hell at someone, no matter how angry you may be, if you truly care about the person in any way, any way at all, do not ever, ever in a million years compare them to the person responsible for heinous, cruel acts to everyone they have ever loved or lived to keep safe. Just don't. Bite your tongue until you taste blood, for words do kill. Of course, she had no clue what evil had transpired directly toward me and other siblings upstairs, as none of us had ever reported anything, and the second floor of the house had been my elder brother's realm with no parental units trespassing beyond the bottom of the stairs in years. Years. Though the cops had. Whole other book.

But she did. She did say it.

And then, as though to ensure the wounds would be fatal, she said it once more in a quiet sword of a slice, her eyes turning to slits of flaming fear and hatred, her lips pulled back so that she appeared as Cruella Deville in my drug clouded brain.

"You're exactly like him." Her voice flattened. Empty. Hollow. Dead. "Get out," she said hoarsely, looking down and shaking her head, exhausted. "Just get out; I never want to see you again."

I gave her the finger and walked out.

I tell you this little story here because it was a long time before I returned to that house, and even longer, more than a decade longer, before I returned to the house to speak in any real way to me mum. When I was there, it was simply to make an appearance, check on my younger sister primarily, although there were plenty of times when I returned, intent to make the impossible work, but these efforts faltered increasingly quickly. So, school? What was that? After this, I would drop in and out of school depending where I was staying, as initially I had some friends who were still attending school, some of them quite seriously, and I would drop into this class or that, audit now and again. There was also the usual networking and business arrangements made before and after school in the various smoking areas and parking lots, as well as intermittently during the day, for the whole school system had swung left and it was pretty loosey, goosey wherever I went. The seventies' high school experience was a far cry from what you currently find. Smoking areas, students' rights, environmental and outdoor clubs, state of the art science departments and off-the-charts art department budgets; there were hip new teachers everywhere with long hair evidently offering students the latest philosophical and political street rants. There were sit ins and free time and no police presence unless someone completely od'd or lost it too badly in some other way. It was a boon if you could be there for it. I couldn't. By then I wasn't anywhere for long stretches of time. There are a couple of clear memories of some of the classes I had attended one way or another however: a cooking class in which we made some killer chocolate chip cookies and then ate them all, a class in Mandarin in which I became aware of ideas unavailable in the English language, an art class wherein I fell into a love triangle with Van Gogh and Georgia O'Keeffe, a mind blowing astronomy class with an actual planetarium and tilt back chairs, an acting class in which I performed a monologue – which for some reason I took from the final chapter of **Atlas Shrugged** and even performed a central part once in a production of **Waiting for Godot**. You know, the one where I spoke from my perch in a trash can.

My primary educational experience during what we in the states call high school years, was far from formal or traditional. What I learned was that life was always willing to offer a lesson and that if I kept my eyes and ears open and was willing to work it, I could accumulate information and knowledge that was simply inaccessible to those who attended school with lessons and teachers in a building every day as though some strange rote meaningless dance they were condemned to enact for being born and growing older in a society that had never made any sense to me. And in this way, my basic educational philosophy was borne. Learning happened everywhere. Everywhere and eternally. It extended beyond that with time of course. My greatest teachers were not in a school; my teachers, other than life itself, were my books and the Asian chefs I worked with at a nearby restaurant. I had developed an unquenchable thirst for reading as a tiny person, due to the patient assistance and consistent modeling of my sister mum and years spent hiding behind the couch to read or in the safety of library stacks as a child. I read absolutely everything. Things not many 13- or 14-year-olds were reading – like **Being and Non Being**, **The Mass of Creation**, **Plato's Republic**, among others. Then I'd go to work, and talk about it with my chef maestros, as well as discuss what else I'd learned from whatever had occurred that day, and I'd ask them questions, because they demanded I ask questions. They were delighted to have such an assiduous student, I can tell you. Though they weren't gonna show me that very often. "Whatcha reading now kid?" Was the standard greeting when I'd walk in the back door and punch my time card into the clock. And you best believe I had been reading, as well as journaling and doodling about what I had read. given that reality, books, and old immigrant chefs were the three pillars of my high school education, I excelled beyond my years in many ways, and I was completely, ridiculously, embarrassingly immature in many others.

A month before I turned 18, I returned from living in the Bay Area and re-entered the world of formal education, this time and for the first time willingly. Although perhaps even more clueless about such a system than I had once been as a wee child. If you had told me the previous autumn that I would be doing such a thing, I would have thought you were tripping out. But the past few months had taken a toll on my psyche. I had lost friends to jail, prison, madness, suicide, and perhaps worst of all, to a sort of vacuous ghost that overtook their bodies and souls and minds and had them now walk about without any light in their eyes. My friends had all manner of rationales for being stuck. I referred to it as the victim act; it made me puke then and it still does. The fact that I was losing friends left, right and sideways, coupled with the urgent demands of my chef teachers to take the ACT exam, had brought me to this juncture. My chef educators were delighted when I aced the literature and writing, and held my own with the mathematics and science. I guarantee you from my own experience alone that anyone working in a kitchen learns math and science; it provides ample lessons in proportion, ratio, measurement, and myriad science studies, most notably the physics and chemistry once known as alchemy. It helps when the chefs are immigrants with degrees in their own countries as doctors and lawyers and physicists. Evidently the test makers and the college admission officers were down with it as well, because here we were, at the rear end of age 17, settling into a dorm room in northern West Virginia, listening to the new Genesis album and waiting for our roommate to arrive.

When it all started, we opted for a major in psychology. This is odd to me because I had known from the age of seven that I wished to be a writer. Writing was my passion, my mainstay, my anchor. I had been writing in some sort of journal or diary daily since I was seven years old and had received a diary as a holy communion gift. I had written poems and stories and lyrics for years. But I imagine I didn't opt to study writing for the same reason many folks didn't and still don't study what they are most passionate about and committed to if it was the arts: artists and writers need to work at a job to survive whilst trying to make their way in the world. This is the United States of America, where everyone must pull their own weight and the societal values demand we all work. And in this country, sadly, in some cases tragically, art is not considered valid work unless you become famous. Period.

I came from what was considered a working class family as did most everyone it seemed back then, and despite everything else that had happened in that arena, the clearest decree was that everyone worked for whatever they got. Nothing came for free. Nothing. Chores began young and only ended when you got out. When I was still a child and I had let my guard down enough to speak truth to the mum and let her know my intentions to be a writer when I grew up, she snapped back that I better study something more practical if I intended to have enough money to live on. That one stuck like a lance in my heart and took up residence in my head.

But this was the mid-seventies and colleges were still operating fairly free form in regard to academics and guidelines. In other words, I could take whatever I wanted as long as I didn't exceed the total of 19 credits I could take for the tuition I paid via school loans and grants and three part time jobs. And so, with little to no guidance of any sort, I signed up for four psych classes, one philosophy class, and a psych lab. Even in this I was odd, though I didn't discover that fact until I started to meet other students in the dorms and dining halls and classes and found out that they were all here on their daddy's dime and had registered for only 12 or 13 credits so they'd have plenty of time to party. I wasn't sure what the party was for and chose instead to head toward the new library building and the stacks which had cradled me through life until then. I did find a few other strange souls by the time winter rolled through; one young man who was determined to become a doctor and help discover a cure for cancer who I lost track of when he graduated early, another who wished to get his law degree and save the world from capitalist madness who ended up dying in the early eighties of AIDs, and another who left one semester for El Salvador before his graduation and was never heard from again by anyone including his family members. So, you see how it was, how I was. Not an average college coed, or whatever they're called. Even the street followed me to college.

But, yet again, it didn't last long anyway for me; that first taste of college life didn't necessarily improve my appetite for more. It was still the seventies, and I still had a penchant for psychedelic substances, and plenty of young folks were still traveling about the country in ratty old vans or standing along the highways with thumbs extended hoping a ratty old van would pass by and stop. So I left that college the next spring, and with three friends in an old car and most of a pound of weed in the trunk we went, for some reason, to Canada, and camped out for some months in Nova Scotia until the snow and cold became too much of a drag, and then we headed back to the states. I learned to drive a stick shift that journey and saw my first silver fox in the moonlight. I also learned that no one outside of the states drank cold beer, the rationale I was offered was that American beer tastes so badly that it needs to be cold to be potable. This mattered to me little though, as I was fortunate not to like alcohol. Give me a joint or shroom any day but people on alcohol just looked stupid and messy to me.

After that, I worked and traveled and went to school to learn what I was interested in wherever I landed. In fact, my college career spanned a little over nine years and occurred in at least five colleges and universities in many very different states throughout the United States. It included the birth of two children and the loss of one. I worked many a shit job as well as some primo ones throughout the US, Puerto Rico, and Canada, none of which ever paid much but I harvested many valuable lessons from each. My college career included more tragedies than celebrations, with the loss of dear friends not an unusual thing in the era of AIDs and drug-induced madness. With the old forms or dictates of family and society no longer available and nothing new yet to fill its niche, there was nothing to hold fast to and so many of us were in free fall. When I finally finished enough of the correctly aligned college courses to warrant a bachelor's degree, I was 25 years old, had an 18-month-old daughter to raise, and a job born out of an internship with a small upstate press. There too, I learned lessons I still use to my own as well as others' benefit.

The four-year post-secondary "education" in the United States is a farce, an illusion, an expensive societal drama at best. Despite the fact that I have no experience myself with paying the tiller so I could take classes in order, get the piece of paper stamped, and get out of wherever, I have attended many classes in many colleges and universities, in bachelor programs, certification programs, and graduate schools, and what I know from experience is that the truly educated folks who come through such a system and either maintain or increase their innate brilliance do so despite their coursework rather than as a result. The folks who obtain a degree in the standard format yet stand out from their peers and ultimately lead throughout society, those who stand out as truly knowl-edgeable in their field as educated persons, usually have done so rooted in and supported by a handful of folks, perhaps only one, living or dead, who were their mentors, their real teachers. These individuals may also be graced to come from a family and school system which offered support and hon-esty and a clear system of ethics in which questioning was highly valued. They accepted responsibility for their own education long ago, usually as small children, and had read and explored and questioned and experienced everything they possibly could to learn everything they possibly could along the way. But these folks are more rare than we ever stop to consider as a society. And their journey through the educational system is not always a pleasant and beneficial one. Not usually.

When I was in a graduate program, I was actually shushed by fellow students, all at least somewhat accomplished professionals in their fields. Shushed. An attempt to shame me into silence. Here was their consistent explanation: The prof lets us go when s/he's done – if you ask a question it just makes the class longer and we want to go home. Seriously? These were professional people in education, social work, medicine, criminal science; the youngest were in their late 20s but the average age was probably in the mid 40s. So evidently it still wasn't about learning anything for real? It still wasn't about learning to improve or deepen one's self? And how real can our structures and systems be when they are simply extensions from a half-baked educational model insistent on defending its stupidest contrivances and ignorance?

Let us stop to consider some further ramifications of what some refer to as the "dumbing down" of America. If, after we have been educated to fill a role in society, we rise above others and are then celebrated in our work places or communities for the achievements, by definition, we literally "stand out" from our peers, yes? We celebrate and honor folks who stand out in this nation when they are simply doing what they said they would do - write a factual story, or teach a child mathematics, or care for the dying. They are enjoying their work, embracing their responsibilities and hardships and possibilities with what is considered unusual zest and determination. But why is such excellence and assiduousness not the standard instead of the exception? Why are we not all taught to strive to develop whatever excellence, brilliance, and talents we carry within ourselves? And why are we not supported by all of society in our learning so we can configure a life for ourselves which best suits us and is therefore most valuable to society? It is sometimes as though we are defending our rights in this country, as individuals and as a nation, to be ignorant and lesser then who we may be, and to be content with whatever slop is served up.

I have oftentimes refused to hire someone who had the usual, necessary requisite or even fancy degrees in both the publishing and educational fields. A bachelors' degree, and some graduate degrees, are strange creatures, acting as though a blind stamp of approval for meeting the basic requirements, when what is necessary is to go out and really learn it in the world. Too often, there is little to no exploration of real world experiences of the studies' tenets until it is all over and the supposed sacred degree has been obtained. And some actually say, too late. I have told student teachers and first year teacher mentees to please forget everything they were taught and to ask students questions rather than assume they knew anything, at least if they wanted to better understand how to teach. This is the litmus test for any career that is more of a calling than a career: do you truly wish to understand the situation regardless of how messy it may get? Enough to try to work with others to improve it? If not, buzzer goes off, choose another option. If a teacher doesn't wish to better understand the students, they are, in fact, not a teacher.

THE ACADEMY EXPERIENCE.

In the late 80s, a primarily self-taught woman, beleaguered with depression and anxiety due to consistent, long term childhood abuse, was working as a successful writer and editor in upstate New York, and remembered a promise she had made to herself as a girl of 13 in south Pittsburgh. In the memory, she sits on a curb along a busy boulevard, her head literally in her crossed arms across her crossed legs; her eyes remain dry. She hadn't wept since she was a tiny child and no longer knew how. But she was praying, though she had no clue about god, or about anything. She was praying to what-ever might listen; she was praying to some part of herself which might survive. She was praying first for someone to notice her, to stop, to ask if she was okay. But she knew deep within that it was an errant prayer and quickly switched from begging to longing, a wishing, a yearning, a hoping. And here is what she stated to herself clearly and deliberately: if I ever make it out of here, if I survive and don't go mad, if I ever figure out what we're doing here, please let me not forget this feeling, this horrible anguish of not knowing anything, of not having anyone who cares or knows anything. Let me be there for those who are lost and searching.

*"Rather than love,
than money, than fame,
give me truth."
- Henry David Thoreau*

In 1989, at age 29, with little formal education of my own and certainly no degrees or certifications in education yet, I had the opportunity to help a bunch of young people start a school in upstate New York. Decades later I asked an excellent therapist, given where I came from, what made me think I could do such a thing? "You survived," was all she said, shrugging a bit. The longer answer is that evidently childhood trauma can leave some strange prints. In many ways, survivors may pull back, lack belief in themselves. In other ways, we have no boundaries or reality checks others may depend on to navigate life. But there is the fact that when we repeatedly survive untenable or potentially fatal situations as a child, we may also see within that experience itself that anything is possible, and live that way at times when it is most beneficial to others.

In the decade that I worked with students at the academy, I never said no to a project idea – even when it was going to cost and require everything. My questions always concerned the why and how. What's the intention, the aim? What's its value to actual learning? And how can we pull it off? What's required and how can we accomplish it? As I write, I realize that this is all too often not investigated in public school classrooms. If ever. Students are not asked what they wish to learn, and if they are, they will either be sarcastic from having not been taken seriously previously, or they'll be told it's not possible. Rarely, rarely do public school teachers get to work with students to discover and design and implement and yes, even celebrate, a true, living, learning experience.

When people ask me why I did such a thing, I often say things like, "I must have been too young to know what the hell I was getting myself into." Yet I remade that initial commitment every single day at 6 am, standing alone in front of the schoolhouse transformed from an old barn or in a circle of others somewhere in New York City or in pouring rain in the high peaks of the 'daks for the next ten years. I would stand every morning at 6 am, take a deep breath, remember the school wasn't mine, and recommit to the effort. A little prayer that I may be useful, helpful, real, true. That was all I ever hoped for; I never wanted to contribute anything to the world that was more surface slathering over, more lies to comfort, more deviation than truth. And so, I prayed every morning that it not be of me, but of something truer, kinder, wiser. And that whatever may be in me that would hinder it would be lost in the effort so that I could become a finer instrument for the divine music I'd heard at times in the deep woods or high desert mesas, that I'd seen in the eyes of the dispossessed more times than not.

Once I remembered, I offered a workshop to some of the local kids hanging out on main street. I held it at a friend's bookstore's upstairs loft space in a multimedia workshop I called Rewriting Creation, which began as an exploration of indigenous creation myths and then snowballed into an entire production that included mask making from whatever clean alleyway trash we could rummage, music inspired by the precursors of "Stomp" and a bunch of rappers, and a culminating creation myth which sought to explain not just the creation of earth and human life, but included the creation of abuse, corruption, racism, etc. It was a hit. They totally rocked it.

Working with one of the young women participants late in the afternoon one summer day, she wondered aloud why they couldn't learn like this all the time? And of course, I didn't turn and explain why that wasn't possible in the American public education system. I just said, I guess we can; we just have to figure out how. And so we did.

I have no clue how it all happened so quickly though. I had to return to college for a semester to complete student teaching while also attending night classes for the missing coursework needed for a provisional teaching license in New York. I had to complete application processes for my license as well as create the even more demanding and lengthy license application for a new non-public school. These are not simple, easy matters in New York state. Then there was the part about where? New York is more often cold and wet than otherwise and though we all ended up spending a great deal of time outdoors regardless of the weather, a schoolhouse where materials can be kept and warmth can be supplied is always a sound investment. I scouted out an old three-story horse barn with a roof caving in, the kiss of death to an old building in the north country, right on the edge of the property where I was living in a Gurdjieff community at the time. The community board agreed to us renting and restoring and using the old barn and the use of the 17 acres surrounding it. This was a real boon, as it provided the school a handful of other adults who were enthusiastic about the project and volunteered much to the initial efforts which demanded demo, construction, and teaching some lessons and workshops. Our first order of business demanded everyone interested in forming a school hold a huge yard sale to replace the roof. We made three grand as I recall; the exact price to repair the roof that year, and therefore stopping further, potentially lasting damage.

By summer's end, one of the parents involved who was an artisan and builder donated a year of his life in trade for room and board and taught us everything he could about building, while transforming a dead barn into a living miracle where other miracles could now occur. That year was a real torment and chain of miracles and certainly deepened my prayer life beyond all previous notions about what was possible. But those kiddos, those first nine, boy did they learn their fractions and angles, as well as some of the reasons we learn them, I'll tell you. They knew the importance of a saved foundation as well as losses and benefits of replacing one; we all learned countless lessons together, lessons which all too often remain unlearned in more static, conventional environments.

In November, having established that the old stone foundation had to go and having spent many days banging at it with a sledge and chanting every poem and song from our repertoire loudly while doing so, we set about to place the forms and pour a new foundation. Then it rained, poured really; the air became water. For three whole weeks the sky streamed. I would climb the ladder set up to climb what was becoming the main hall of the old building which we now had perched upon a few pressurized jacks, and at two or three in the morning after working for hours on administrative crap, with the rain and wind howling and screaming like a banshee, I would just stand there, the barn frame rocking like old Noah's ark on the high seas, and yes, I would pray. Let it be okay; let me be okay. I'm pretty sure I had moments of horrifying clarity where I saw more fully what I was getting myself into; it was always coupled with a terror that I was an imposter, that I knew nothing, that I would most certainly fail. But I could have had no idea of the reality I was stepping into. Like any new bride or groom heading off into a new life, a new world, we can never know until it is often too late. The commitment has been made; the life must be lived.

Meanwhile, while I prayed through my terror and hope, the students put together a time capsule with their original poems and little pieces of late 80s Americana to place into the front of the new cement foundation. At a certain point we simply tired of waiting. Several of the young women heavily invested in the school and a couple of their mums came over in the wee morning hours and helped. We literally pushed the thick, muddy water out of the forms with our first bare, then mud caked arms and hands as we sang and grunted and laughed. We had called the cement company earlier that week for a delivery and we were ready when they arrived. The sky cleared. Omens are everywhere when we quit looking and dig deeper.

The first year of the school's functioning, I rented the "meditation room" in the community farmhouse next door to the horse barn aka schoolhouse. We worked inside when the weather demanded but spent as much time outdoors as possible. There was no furniture, nor money for it, which did not seem problematic at all given my tendency to sit cross legged on the floor and the student's to curb squat. Besides, there were plenty of meditation cushions of all persuasions readily available. No one complained.

My memories of the first year involve more chaos than clarity.

I had nine children ages 11 through 13 as students when we began with what I called an integrated thematic study. I figured a good place to begin would be to get oriented in regard to where we were - geographically, historically, etc. - so we studied "The World". We studied world geography, recreating it in clay and paper mache' models which we hung everywhere as reference points; we hiked woods and streams and wetlands to discover hidden reminders of who else shared the land and waters with us and who had been here before us; we studied the Fibonacci sequence and the golden proportion and pursued all of the mathematical and artistic and musical studies that derived from it. We built loch ness monsters and other mystical beasts from the snow, (always plentiful there), for the students to play on once they iced up overnight or the large tree carcasses also plentiful down in the wood in the warmer months. We studied and sang rounds and folk songs from various places and times throughout the world and learned about specific cultural values through them. We went on herbal walks, found plants growing beneath the snow, and learned a bit about what the old healers knew and why they were burned as witches post scientific revolution. We played with common words, their origins, and how the words and world had changed together, often also changing each other. And of course, we helped with the building whenever possible. In fact, by mid-winter, we were using what came to be known as the "main hall", long before it had windows or any other finish work.

As a "culminating project" for our studies, students opted for a renaissance-type faire. We built a renaissance village out of huge cardboard refrigerator boxes, duct tape, and paint, and held a small faire replete with jugglers, face painting, and other side shows for parents, friends, and the larger community. Each student determined the role they would don in our little homemade village. After much discussion and research, they designed their little cardboard shops, and, after we thoroughly ravaged the local appliance stores for boxes, it was construction time! There was a cobbler, a woodworker, a baker, an herbalist, a tarot reader, and even a surgeon-barber. It was a huge hit and as the years progressed, more and more folks were drawn to our public presentations and events. I never took out an advert anywhere. Word of mouth was all that was needed in what was then a small New York town.

Our initial little band of nine willing learners had gathered from several very different places and were joined by several others as the year progressed. Some students lived in the small community I was a member of at the time, some arrived after completing studies in a local Waldorf school where I had taught grammar through poetry in exchange for my own daughter's education costs the previous year, and there were also students who came to the school as a transition, which was something that continued to occur throughout the decade the school community existed and flourished. One student had been home schooled by her mother but her mother had recently died and her father was wise enough to know that sending her off to junior high at the public school would have been tantamount to cruelty. So he brought her to us. And of course they had no money.

Not many people who need immediate help due to trauma have money.

Another student came in with his mum for an interview after we had started things up. He too had been home schooled, though his family's version of home schooling was the variety that gives home schooling everywhere a bad name. He woke at noon after playing video games all night while his folks, both artist musician types in Woodstock, partied on. I am not sure what woke the parents up enough to come in and make an effort to do right by their son, most likely the school district or even state wondering what was up, but I can tell you it did not pan out as a long-term commitment. There were other students who arrived throughout the year, as word spread of a new educational opportunity for teenagers in a county where the only nonpublic school options were a parochial school or one of the expensive private schools across the river. The academy experience predated charter schools in New York and was never able to apply to become one as we'd been up and running for six years before charter schools were introduced, and in New York a functioning school was not able to apply for the designation and the dollars which would follow. Though I am not sure we would have applied in any case. We wanted the state licensure so students could have more options available further down the road, but what they would have had as stipulations and demands if we'd opted for charter school designation most likely would have deterred us.

Ultimately, due to the societal supplication of school licensure, at a certain point, likely due to the then current educational farce known as No Child Left Behind, the state changed the regs for "licensed non public schools" which demanded all of our students now take all the stupid state exams to prove they knew the basic material all potential good citizens must know. Turned out it wasn't much of a dilemma for most of our young folks as they blew them away one by one, frequently a couple of years before their peers in public school. Given that our primary academic focus for students was on truly learning, thinking and questioning and expressing themselves, they were prepared to sit for whatever imbecilic exams our society demands to do just about anything. We were able to work on test taking skills with those who suffered from test anxiety, and we were able, as it turned out, to go ahead with our curriculum designs and simply spend a couple of weeks prior to the state exams drilling each other on the material and taking practice exams. Still, it was yet another hurdle delivered by society to make it harder for us to just focus on learning how to be the best human beings we could become.

When I designed the school on paper, the basic philosophy involved engaging as many of the students' faculties in the learning as possible and exploring connections rather than divisions. I also held firmly to the notion that without actually creating something based on what was just learned, no knowledge would actually be attained or integrated and would soon be forgotten. This was the basis for absolutely every study and often the smaller aspects of a study, to culminate in a creative project and to be chronicled constantly in their journals and ultimately in their increasingly fat portfolios. However, in my view, as stated in the piles of documents I had to write for the school's initial certification application, I was not merely interested in the education of minds, no matter how creatively taught. I wanted to allow people a safe place in which to come alive, to discover who they were in the world and invest in themselves, to wake up, to wake each other up. I wanted them to see we are all connected, to absolutely everything, and that we all reflect each other. I wanted them to see that without presence, without awareness and mindfulness, all is for naught. I wanted them to see they could do more than survive; they could thrive. And I wanted them to know through and through that, in fact, it is a primary human responsibility to do so.

In New York state at that time, the application process for a "non-public school" demanded one obtain a provisional license, and after three years of operating as a school, making sure to keep the fee payments and paperwork up to date with the state, begin the application for permanent licensure, which is more paperwork and money, and also included the promise of a visit from an official from the office of non-public schools' from the New York State Education Department in Albany. When the school hit the three-year mark, I went ahead and applied for the permanent licensure and we all began to work assiduously to put all the paperwork in order for the state rep.

Our official arrived early one morning and joined us for circle after which I was too busy to worry about him much and so I handed him off to a student and told him to feel free to explore as he wished. When I found him a couple of hours later, he was sitting at a table in the attic work space with a bunch of students who were all very busy with their work – writing, painting, discussing, bouncing ideas off of each other, asking the official all manner of questions – gawd only knows. But when I approached and apologized for my absence, he looked up with a Cheshire grin and shook his head; he was having a great time.

"Would you like to see the paperwork now?" I asked him.

"Oh," he responded looking lost for a moment. "Paperwork?" He scanned the room once more slowly, as though ingesting it as much as possible. "Oh, I don't need to see any paperwork," he allowed. I must have looked rather uncertain as he quickly added, "What's going on here wouldn't really fit on paper would it?" he said.

I followed his gaze, looking around at the students working. Not many were primarily interested in what we were discussing. They had their own focuses and were engaged in learning and creating and exploring ideas together. Who were we adults who imagined ourselves so important? It mattered not, as long as they could continue. Evidently, they trusted me to handle the pesky details. I had no response other than a smile to meet his. He stood up and we shook hands warmly, eye to eye.

"Look," he said, "there's no problem with this school obtaining permanent certification immediately and that will be my formal recommendation to the state."

Now the students nearby perked up, as those with peripheral antennae began to understand who this was and what was at stake and whispered to each other to shush. He looked around at the students throughout the attic room who were all engaged, busy, attentive, alive, and learning, and he made a sweeping gesture with his arms to include the entire place and everyone in it.

"What you have here is magic," he said, "This is unprecedented; I've been at this a long time and I've never seen anything like it in my life." Of course, the students all had to start cheering and hugging him and patting him on the back. He saw us; he got us; and best of all perhaps, especially for those of us living in fear of once again being dismissed by "the man", he approved. We were all beyond relieved and joyous. But he didn't linger; he was long gone by midday circle and our lunch in which we always served each other first, thus negating the necessity to selfishly pile up our own plates first.

At the academy, we began and ended each day in circle, singing songs and reciting poems, journaling and sharing and making announcements. Throughout the day, we made a point of taking time to look into each other's eyes when we were handing someone something or we spoke with each other; we paused and reconnected to our senses at every transition; we practiced yoga and meditation and breathing exercises at every turn. I would warn them not to grow up and become the people who had buttons or raisins for eyes and no one ever asked me to clarify that statement. They already knew, by the age of 11 or 13 or 15, that there were plenty of folks out there claiming to be adults who had forfeited their hearts and souls, and they also knew they did not wish to become like them. It was, in fact, why many of them were here. I reminded them often that those who amass money and power and status often must forfeit something precious in return and I also suggested that we may have enough of these folks roaming the planet already and need not yield and supply society with more. I warned them of the common worm hole in which self-importance replaced self-awareness throughout our academic and professional fields. Many had already been branded deeply by those pretending to know something when ignorant, defending their ignorance with further lies. The academy supplied them with an alternative model.

One of the most critical, fruitful, lasting practices which I had implemented at the very beginning and which continued throughout the life of the school and beyond that for some students was our morning journal time. We began the day in circle, not standing, but sitting. Sitting on the floor of the main hall and writing in our journals, we would pour out the nonsense along with the daily fears and last night's dreams along with the more existential ponderings and share them with each other after we all wrote. At that point we knew it as journaling from our own experience, and it had recently been dubbed "free-writing" by the academic world. Now, most folks refer to the practice as "the morning pages"; this change occurred after Julie Cameron wrote **The Artist's Way** in 1991 and popularized the practice. Journaling first thing had so many advantages for so many people in so many ways it isn't possible to begin to list them even partially. However, I believe the most essential was the daily opportunity to share one's ideas, feelings, and voice with others in a safe place which cultivated everyone's attention and awareness as well as cementing the school community.

The practice changed in small ways as it evolved along with the school and the students. There were times I or another person in circle would offer a reading as a focus or put a quote on the board (sometimes in backwards writing just for fun) or we may just truly free write whatever was churning through in the moment. Regardless of the method used, the practice itself always held fast to all of us there and we held to it, some of us as a life saver amidst a turbulent storm in life; for some, the practice would be utilized to process trauma and/or create throughout their adult professional lives. It was and continues to be one of the primary practices always cited by my former students and their folks as valuable, even critical, for the positive changes the student made.

We'd been up and running for quite a few years when we were joined by a young man of twelve who had spent the first six years of his schooling at his own desk in the principal's office. He evidently had been diagnosed with ADHD (a new diagnosis available at that time, clarifying and adding another aspect to the previously blankettingly available ADD) and was on a great deal of medication. When we met as part of the application process, he claimed he couldn't read or write; he was visibly and audibly angry at the entire universe. When I asked him and his folks if it was possible to titrate him off the meds before the school year began, and try to handle his needs in other ways during the day, to see what alternatives may be possible, they were more than happy to give it a try. Neither liked the side effects suffered by their son from these meds. Given that he would rarely be expected to sit still and never need to sit quietly at a desk in a row of others, doing what everyone else was doing, I suggested it may not be necessary at all. Medications can work their magic; they are sadly just as likely to be thrown at folks inappropriately by the many inept psychiatrists and physicians out there wanting to keep the peace for whomever is paying their fee without ever taking the time to understand or to learn about the actual human being in front of them. Our primary replacements for his drugs? He had the option, at any time or any point in the day, to run down to the stream to see if the great blue heron we'd named Ezmerelda was down at the creek near the little wooden bridge. He could run through the wood like a wild man if he felt it was what he needed. He could reach out to a teacher or older student for help whenever needed. And he had a supply of caffeine drinks should he need to reverse a rush that wouldn't leave him alone no matter what. He was dubious but willing; his folks were happy as hell.

One snowy morning, everyone walked in as usual, kicked their outdoor shoes and boots into the cubbies in the foyer, hung up their wet coats, and shuffled or ran or danced into circle in the main hall. We'd been working together for a few months as this particular group of folks so everyone not only knew each other, some were more like siblings and there were of course, regardless of efforts made to speak openly about sexual matters, teenaged humans with raging hormones and no cultural narratives left to cling to in the storms, and so there were the tentative or passionate romances and broken hearted dramas now and again. However, we also had a solid core of well-seasoned students in the circle who made sincere efforts openly to become more aware and the real boon to that was that these guys and gals were considered "cool" by their younger counterparts, affording them and their efforts far more weight for the rest of the students to cling to in place of their own, usually long lost, cultural heritage.

And then, there he was, one of our newest and neediest recruits sliding into his spot in the circle, closest to the door. He just sat there, his folded journal stuck out from one of his back pockets, no pen or pencil in sight, scowling as he sat with his knees bent, arms crossed around them, his head resting on his knees. Fetal comfort. It was mid-November and he had yet to join in the morning journal writing. I had talked about it with him individually several times; I had told him he could simply draw. Student journals were considered sacred and were pulled out to be used in all sorts of situations where writing may be beneficial – they were not "corrected" but responded to with questions and thoughts and related experiences shared with the student such that both their writing and their thinking may become more clear or structured or whatever it was that the student may have as an intention for their journaling. But he could not yet know all of this, for he had yet to venture toward a single written word. Like so, so many students from or in a formal school setting, he was afraid, even terrified perhaps, of getting it wrong again and being made fun of or even being dismissed entirely. The solution to getting it wrong is simple; don't do it. A logical solution to the ongoing dilemma that had worked until now.

And yet, today, as I looked up from my own journaling to sweep the room and check in on folks, I could tell he wasn't as dissociated from himself and what was going on in the circle as he had been; he was engaged enough to peer up and out of his self-made womb and look around at the other students to at least begin to see what was going on.

If I see an opening to a possibility, I have to make the effort to realize that possibility. And so I put my journal down and went over to where he sat, slumped in circle, and sat to his left (he was a lefty) and a bit behind him and the student next to him. "What's up?" I whispered.

He pulled a common pubic school move, looking up at the ceiling as though searching for something. Ah yes, sarcasm, the lowest and most abundant form of humor in the US. Without turning to look at me he whispered back. The rest of the students were either too involved in their own writing to notice me there or knew that it was none of their business since I hadn't addressed him aloud in circle to include everyone in the discussion. They were a well-seasoned bunch he had joined, including a couple of guys aged 16 and 17 who were as genuine and assiduous in their efforts as anyone I'd met in life thus far.

"Lights in the ceiling?" he stage whispered as though wonder struck.

"What's up?" I repeated, same neutral tone, same whisper level. Nothing new or exciting to fuel his resistance or fear.

He turned and tried to level me with a glare. I leveled him back with neutral, unconditional acceptance. He disengaged his eyes and turned his back to me. Then he started muttering bitterly, mimicking my own question and responding with diverse answers. "Air." "Outerfuckinspace." "The ceiling." "The goddamned attic." "The sun."

Then he ran out of steam. I was quiet for a moment, listening to him breathe as well as the sounds of other students stirring. The other students had begun to finish up and were sitting quietly waiting for everyone to finish so we could share some of our writing, or were going out quietly to pee or grab something from the attic they would need after circle. They all knew enough to move quietly and pay no attention to what I was up to with the young man.

"Listen," I said, perusing the room, "I've used up all your journaling time so why don't you just think of one word and rewrite it over and over again while the other students are reading to the group? No one is gonna notice. Just try it to see what happens, as an experiment." I tossed a pen in front of him rather than ask and got up immediately as it required a written or not written response; I wasn't going to give him a chance to respond with the same old, same old verbal crap.

I went to my own empty spot in circle, sat down quietly, closed up my own journal and just watched and waited quietly until everyone else was ready. I could see him peripherally. Our young recruit was struggling inside enough that it was visible. I smiled inside without any visible signs. He needed no more fuel. He needed to decide whether to battle this out within himself now.

After about the third person had read aloud and shared from their own writing, he began to write, slowly initially, and then gaining speed, trying to fill a page with a single word. He stopped before the others were done reading so I looked around the circle at each face to see who was waiting for a more personal invitation to read. Not everyone is gregarious or confident, poised to share aloud; many need to be invited personally, especially those newly arrived from public school or timid with their own writing or ideas. I invited those who had yet to share to do so and most of them opted to go for it. Then it was just him who had yet to be invited. He had written, so he had something to share. I knew he had plenty to share, ultimately, the poor kiddo was both brilliant and deeply sensitive in a society not interested in either.

I looked at him until he looked up at me. "Have anything to share today sir?" I asked, allowing just a shmidgeon of my hope to be heard amidst the primarily neutral tone. He hesitated enough that I added, "All good either way; your call."

"It's just one word over and over," he said. "It's stupid."

Another student quipped, "Unless the word is actually 'stupid'", she said, "You owe the justice jar a quarter." She smiled and laughed to let him know she was just being a smart ass. He rolled his eyes, no stranger to adding quarters to the jar at this point anyway. Or sarcasm.

Then one of the "cool" older guys who always wrote voluminous verses fraught with clarity and imagination spoke up. "Hey," he yelled over to the uncertain 12-year-old, throwing his fist in the air for added power, "go for it!" He nudged his best bud next to him in the ribs and smiled; his pal and fellow student was a genius musician, literally. Sadly, at age 17, he was just beginning to realize his own possibilities.

The nudge worked; reawakening his bud enough to join in. "Yeah," his buddy responded to the young man rather than his friend. "We gotjer back man." He winked at the younger student and smiled his long ago earned stoner's grin.

The young man's uncertainty was becoming resolve in front of our eyes. He opened his journal to the first page and looked at it blankly, then read a few lines silently, mouthing the word, then stood up. "What the hell," he muttered. They had tossed him a suit of armor and a horse and reminded him they were there beside him, weaponed and ready. He could go fully into battle now, well-brothered.

"snowsnowsnowsnowsnowsnow," he began muttering with a bitter edge to his voice.

The musician began a slight beat on the floor with his bare hands, offering him a structure to put the words into that would allow more clarity. His buddy joined in, echoing the beat with his own open palms on the floor. Now everyone was smiling, making some sort of sounds as though sending out tiny life preservers. Now the newest reader on the block was matching their simple beat with his word, varying the tone and loudness and intensity based on fellow students' soundings, asking it as a question, yelling it as though an answer in a quiz show, he read and read. "Snoooooooow, Snow, snow, Snow? Snow! Snoooooooooow. Snow, snow, snow? Snow!" It had quickly become a rap tune. The reader was now beaming, reading, tapping his foot, feeding the whole circle with his effort and his joy. I lived for this alchemy. Wherever there is fear visible, there is always grace available as well.

The student people were just as kind in teaching me. Unfortunately, for the first couple of years, I found myself sometimes at a loss and relying on more traditional methods – a traditional delivery of information if you will - and determining what the students had gotten from the material using a sort of whittled down Socratic method. You know, standard practices. Standard perspectives and stances. I taught them the facts, even told stories to illustrate of course, but essentially, that old "I knew something and I was going to share it" attitude all over everything. They were supposed to get it and be able to prove they got it. But of course I learned far more than they did, for they were better teachers than I, and I was a better student, for I was hungrier to learn and was evidently there to inspire enthusiasm to learn as much as anything else.

There is a scene from that time I recall in great detail in which I am attempting for some reason to teach about the French revolution, which became an excellent lesson for me, and eventually for the students as well. In fact, it became its own revolution. Fortunately, I was often aware of how clueless I was about what I was doing and worked assiduously against "the imposter syndrome". Common among humans everywhere, you may recognize it as the inner voice which insists you are an imposter at whatever you may be engaged in, and it warns spookily that your ruse shall certainly be discovered, and spirals down the proverbial toilet from there. But I was as committed to this adventure as any I had ever embarked upon, so it was possible to not just change the plan when beneficial, but to change my thinking as well. I was clueless but determined. And I was not the kind of person unwilling to admit defeat; mine was the opposite dilemma, I had admitted defeat so often by age 30 that it had become a bad habit or a polished skill, depending on the situation.

I was not invested in living a lie, and therefore I had to live as though what we were claiming was possible, was possible. I had to live it. But I had never intended to contribute to the societal mess myself, nor did I intend to prepare students to do so, so there wasn't any option. The status quo was not merely suspect; as far as I was concerned, from what I had seen of the world in a couple of decades, it was poison to passion and creative ventures and genuine human connection. It had, in most every case, already dismissed me and these children, judging us each and all as too weird or bad or off or wrong or strange. I often pointed out the windows of the school toward town while referring to the "unreal world", the world where truth mattered less than whatever personalities were on parade at the time, whatever ego of the hour needed bolstering. I wanted them to know who they were intrinsically in this world, and what on earth they were doing here. Or, at the very least, to discover they were not alone with their existential questions. So when one of the students copped an attitude with me one day while I was "teaching" about revolution, I turned and asked him what was up. Without an attitude. I really wanted to know. I knew what I was doing wasn't working for any of us and I knew, if given a genuine option, he would somehow share throw me the rope I needed to change things up. He didn't disappoint.

"This sucks," he said simply and honestly.

"Yes," I agreed with him wholeheartedly, "But what would you do differently? How would you teach the information in a way that makes it more pertinent and alive to everyone here?"

Had I been busy defending my techniques, nothing new or relevant would have been possible. I cannot stress this point enough. Teachers and parents busy defending themselves and all the ideas they identify with and that they attach to themselves, allows nothing real to emerge. It's a dead horse that has already been beaten beyond recognition. Instead, we sat down in a circle and brainstormed about ways we could all learn the information and of course it was much better, with the students creating a game using peanut m&ms to act out what had occurred before, during, and after the French revolution. Whalah. Real learning requires only two things - a teacher willing to question openly and students willing to delve into their own creative spirits.

The circle was without a doubt the most critical element of the school. It was certainly the center, and as such it changed size, migrated, and was used as the basic school construct, replacing a more linear, blocky format for everything, including curriculum which tended toward connectivity rather than splintering into specialties. The "societies", primarily indigenous, that still have a connection with nature and their own cultures have not and do not continue to miseducate; they have not forced their young to see and act in the world as though rational order and straight lines matter more than all else. They continue to gather in circles to process matters or celebrate. Lines are not drawn as boundaries which must not be crossed, but are used instead to create a design or dance to a beat. Though we gathered "formally" in the morning, midday, and afternoons daily in circle no matter where we were or what we were doing, anyone in the school could call a circle at any time, and smaller circles often met to make plans or share information within smaller groups working on a project or lesson together.

The circle arrangement of gathering was not an imposed structure. As human beings, as part of a much vaster nature, we naturally congregate in circles. Watch any group of folks - from youngsters to elders – wherever we see humans gather together informally - and you will see it occur naturally, the circles form themselves with us, they host us. Think about it, from toddler reading circles and support groups and quilting circles and football teams planning and rich ladies at afternoon tea and musicians practicing and just about every other scene in life wherein folks are gathering as a group; this formation allows everyone to see everyone else clearly and there is therefore an opportunity for far more learning and open communication.

To sit in arranged seating, all rows and files, and to walk in single or double files, are behaviors which must be learned and therefore taught. To stand in lines and process orderly rather than rumble together like an upturned bin of peanuts requires years of training. Ask any teacher of children under the age of seven. Some of us are more adept at this skill than others, some more into teacher pleasing than others, some wiggle it over themselves like a new uncomfortable skin. And there are those of us who simply refuse to learn it. There are those of us who are actually unable to submit to becoming yet another dot on a line, who want nothing to do with the insane and unnatural feeling of imposed order, who shrink and squirm at first and ultimately, who disappear into their own isolation or anger. You all know us from way back. We're the ones in time out, detention, suspension, jail, psych wards, morgues. Poor thing, people say, never found their way. At best, it's a cruel, rigged system for folks whose natures and intellects don't fit into what already exists, and there are no other options presented. Ask any ten-year-old, or simply try to remember back to that time; "fit in or die" is the rule.

And there are also those of us who do not succumb or revolt or hide. And some of these folks are fairly famous for accomplishments that rise like the Phoenix from the ashes of every battle they have had to wage to hold onto themselves amidst an inhumane system. Consider some who simply went their own way; rather than "fitting in", they made the box much vaster, less boxy even. These folks include historical figures such as Albert Einstein, Margaret Mead, Temple Granden, Charles Darwin, and even George Washington.

More recently, Americans who rose above and beyond the demands to acclimate and become extraordinary people include Stevie Wonder, Keanu Reeves, Adam Levine, Justin Timberlake, Karina Smirnoff, Tom Cruise, Cher, and many others you may be surprised to learn about.

Many years after I had left the school and moved on to other lands and studies, I had the opportunity to do some research regarding resiliency studies focusing on people in their teens and early twenties. The volumes written by various researchers all stated the same conclusion: it only takes one person to make a difference. And it can be anyone - parent, teacher, minister, neighbor, coach, boss – anyone who steps outside the usual negativity or derision the child has been surrounded by long enough that it has now overtaken their own psyche; anyone who consistently shows the child that s/z/he are valuable, that the world has lied to them, that they do matter, that they are indeed valuable.

Anyone with a rational mind may wonder how many of these outstanding minds we have lost in our nation due to our ineptitude and the lack of awareness or kindness within our educational system, as well as all other systems. I personally know several young people whose inner anguish became so overwhelming they took their own lives. Each one a tragic and deep loss not simply to those of us who loved them, but to the entire society which had dismissed them, for they all had gifts to share unavailable anywhere else that are now lost to us all, forever.

At the academy, we gathered in circle to open and close the school day, despite the fact that many students were there in the school or somewhere on the grounds long before and long after the formal day began and ended. Once we had journaled, we sang songs, delivered messages, brought up concerns or possible projects, and recited poetry in our opening as well as closing circles. As the years went along and each person who joined the circle brought their favorites with them, we amassed quite a collection of recitations and songs we could share together. We gathered again in circle midday to share food and eat, always stopping to gather our wits with a simple awareness practices and recite a poem or prayer acknowledging our gratitude for whatever we were having that day, physical food as well as the finer, more substantial foods of attention and learning and creating. We gathered in circles to teach, offer instructions, share our ongoing work, design projects, sketch out the day, and on and on. Once we had a faculty, we met in circle, as did the board of directors and every other group that formed. However, I will admit that my favorite use of the circle was initiated by the students, and it was a delightfully rebelliously public display of possibilities.

We journeyed together as much as we could, beginning and ending every term with a backpacking or canoeing or beach camping journey. In between, since we utilized many community resources in the form of scientists and artists and politicos and academics and farmers, we visited folks to learn what they knew about a specific subject by working alongside them on a specific project. Or we would go to see a specific show at a museum or presentation hall. We also increasingly designed and implemented thematic studies which demanded from their core the need for journeying – thematic studies such as Intentional Community, The Appalachian Trail, Indigenous Mexico, Hudson River, and others demanded we journey to the source to learn as much as possible. And so we did.

Now, we had no money of course. There were eventually a small number of students attending whose folks were able to pay full tuition, but it was a sliding scale arrangement and folks got to say what they could afford. We set our salaries up in August by meeting in a circle as a faculty and hearing how little was projected to be coming in financially that year and then saying aloud what our absolute rock bottom figure was for living expenses. I always went last and took what was remaining, until the last year, when I simply couldn't afford it any longer. Then we would set up the budget by what was feasible economically for the school community folks. It wasn't ever enough for basic staff salaries so the extras were truly extra and we had to actually make the "extra" money.

This need to fundraise was a constant, always fruitful, sideline and I complicated it by refusing to approve the selling of or participation in anything that was counter to what we were all working so hard to create. In other words, we never sold chocolate or chatkees. But we did wash many a car, and we did sell and plant literally thousands of tulip bulbs; perhaps the most consistent fundraiser was a monthly Friday morning litter-a-thon in the downtown area of a nearby college town. This was evidently such a success that it still occurs in that town, more than twenty years after the school closed its doors forever, and is now supported by various other community groups. By the time a few years went by we had pulled together enough money to buy an old small-framed school bus and convert it into a cozy travelling outpost for journeys throughout the United States. The rebellious circles originated from within this bus. Landing in large, public parking lots were a favorite.

We made frequent stops when journeying together. On shorter journeys there were always the pee and coffee and fueling stops; on longer ones we needed to stop at various stores for groceries and other items along the way. Whether we were in cars or in the bus, we all had to eventually pile out and circle up to make sure everyone knew what was happening next and dole out specific responsibilities if needed. But the teacher people didn't direct the formation of the circle as we piled out. It was not our circle, but theirs, for they were, after all, the ones of which the circle was primarily comprised. The students were, literally, the living circle. At a given point, students began to become aware of the power they wielded as a circle of young people chanting out lengthy recitations or singing Sweet Honey and the Rock harmonies or Lakota chants at full volume in public, drumming on and with whatever may be available and hopefully appropriate. People (potential consumers) stopped and turned completely around to stare on their way into the grocery or hardware store; startled by a bunch of grungy dread-haired teens belting out a Shaker round or few pages of Whitman, they turned around, gaped, astonished, then, often, smiled. The students loved it; couldn't get enough

I have to admit I may have loved it more than anyone else. Such a simple lesson. Why fear and fight an invisible force of youthful zest? Why turn aside from such rebellious energy? Why not instead afford opportunities for them to learn to use it wisely and responsibly? Why not let our young people wake us up from our sleepy mindlessness? Why not learn from them some essential human aspect we adults have already forfeited and lost? Not I. I joined in, almost always singing off key and not caring a whit.

The school, like all rich experiences, transformed as it went, and it certainly transformed me. I was not some experienced teacher who had amassed files of ideas with lots of theories to draw from to concoct the perfect learning experience. I really only knew one thing when I began, but it served me and everyone who came through the school well: I knew I did not know. Now, three decades later, now, I know that this is an intellectual stance that actually allows the most learning to occur. However, I did know a few other things. I knew that there were children out there suffering, some of them to the point of suicide, because they were more sensitive or brilliant or just different in some way than the average "normal" person, and because of this, because of who they were, who they were born as, because of their intrinsic selves, they were summarily and constantly dismissed, taunted, bullied, omitted, and discarded. I knew this from the inside out. I also knew all that was needed was to create and cultivate a place of acceptance and kindness. That's what I knew, what I had seen so far in life and learned. And as it turned out, without ever intending to make a certain rule or law, kindness became the orientation for all our behavior, eventually becoming known as "the only rule". Kindness to self as well as others, for by the time we are teens, many of us have learned our lack of worth so well we are already adept at diminishing and denouncing ourselves habitually, at every turn, verbally and physically. I believe this is due to the fact that in our society, in almost every situation, the victim must carry the shame and guilt of the crimes perpetrated against them. The more the heart is rent open, the deeper the wounds, the more profound the shame. This must change. It must change everywhere. (Most recently and societally, we can witness this need at the heart of Black Lives Matter movement, the folks with disabilities demanding their rights, as well as the scrambling of the good old boys to maintain their stance born of fear.)

What I knew about circles came primarily from long ago during my time as a little hippie. Hanging out in the woods and streets, wherever we gathered, around a fire, a pipe, or an idea, safety and acceptance always seemed to be silently mandated as vital and constant elements of the circles I found myself within. And so, I suppose I had anticipated the safety it could provide. What I had forgotten, and what emerged from our circles as well as every other one I have ever been a part of, was the creation and cultivation of a place in which we were able to ground ourselves and move forth in the world more sustained and inspired no matter where we were or what we were doing.

Initially, as I was the only one there over the age of 13 and had practiced such things for more years than that, I led the circle. As a primary facet of that responsibility, I held the circle as sacred. You may wonder what the hell that means, "hold the circle as sacred"? What? Some new age flimsy notion? Some crap where ya burn incense and intone the gawds? Well, not exactly. The word sacred has gotten a bad reputation from misuse I'm afraid, as have many other essential human terms and aspects in recent history. I guarantee you there is nothing flimsy or glitzy or hip about holding a circle sacred, or attempting to do so. Actively holding the circle sacred requires just about everything a person can muster and yet, can eventually be done by everyone who has truly participated in the circle.

Keeping the circle sacred refers to an effort to be aware of everyone in the circle as fully as possible at all times, individually and concurrently. And, at the same time, to also be aware of ones' self – or at least some of the thoughts and emotions and standard neurotic triggers and behaviors that move through us as constantly as our blood flows and nerve endings synapse. It demands one work to respond rather than react; to listen for the truth and feed that, draw upon that, develop that, rather than grab at whatever random, automatic, negative or mindless crap will also always be spouted. Keeping a circle sacred means intuitively reading what may be needed by everyone in every moment and responding as truthfully as possible so it may be fruitful to as many as possible. Do we need a song? Silence? Movement? Discussion? Action? Sharp word? Metaphor? Reminder? Organization? Each moment and every moment. Now and now and now. Working in this way, making this effort, hones one like any focused practice hones a musical instrument. It is trued, if you will. And yes, It is simultaneously excellent and terrifying.

As the principal holder of the circle over the years, I also had to learn a facet of unconditional love I had always resisted, which I refer to as tough love. Leading anything allows us humans to develop in many ways, but from my own experience and what I have seen in the larger, less real world, it involves only one of two avenues. One either truly serves, which means all ideas and notions about yourself and the world that you previously valued are up for grabs and you must consistently step forward into the internal and external changes required, or, you can don some shade of megalomania and become someone very different than who you set out to be. We have all seen the latter scenario more times than we care to recall, in our own lives as well as in others'. My central task, giving the students what they each and all needed in any given moment, demanded a willingness to tell them, sometimes abruptly, to knock off whatever mindless, previously-taped segment of life they were busy idealizing or defending in the moment. I could be very sharp if it was needed, and that went against every idea I myself owned and held precious regarding myself and kindness. It was at times agonizing.

Thinking back, I believe it took a couple of years before I had any consistent reprieve with leading circle, though there were times when one of the students would manage to pull it off as they made their own efforts to grow some awareness. It was these students, the ones willing to risk whatever they had known previously to grow into a person of integrity, who eventually became what I called the "critical mass" of the school. These were the drivers and inspirers and managers; the movers and shakers. Once we had some critical mass in circle, which meant more than just me making concerted efforts at allowing and maintaining some semblance of awareness and holding myself accountable; the effort of leading the circle, holding it sacred, became much, much easier for me.

It was a safe, dynamic place, not really a place at all, but an arrangement of reality if you will, a sort of sacredization of a group of folks within a community of beings for the sole purpose of working together to transcend perceived limitations. We circled up to defy society by becoming as fully ourselves as possible, and the circle of humans trying to become themselves became a cervix through which we, as a group, birthed our studies, journeys, inner realizations, creative projects, discussions, meals, truth telling, ceremonies, dreams unwoven; any and all possibilities could be and often were birthed forth from our circles. There was something so safe and sacred about our circles that just about anything could, and often would be investigated and resolved.

This did not always happen in kumbaya fashion though. You know this, yes? Truth telling is not always pretty and cozy and warm. It can require cutting and get very messy. The stronger and safer the circle was, the more truth we could expose within ourselves and share with each other. And the more we could call each other on our shit – not because it pissed us off, but because we genuinely cared about the person and they knew it. This is a critical piece. Should anything be born out of one's personal discomfort, it is immediately useless or worse. Every word, every suggestion and question, must be born from a genuine love and care or it will just go downhill into the same dark place too many were already hiding within.

There is a marvelous and poignant experience we all shared at midday circle once in which I, despite having led so much for so long, was relieved and overjoyed to simply witness. We, as the students were also involved in the interviewing and hiring process, had hired another full-time teacher person about four years into the school's existence as word had spread far and wide and there were more young folks needing help than I felt I could reasonably handle on my own. The students were also increasingly older, which is what happens naturally when they are fed and watered, and they needed a teacher better versed in the higher, deeper mathematics and sciences that I had to work way too hard to understand and master well enough to teach.

We had had other part time teacher people along the way, many of whom volunteered, some who were bartering, and others who were paid actual money. They each were there to offer something specific and came in and out according to the schedules they'd created with students. Early on, we had a woman from the city philharmonic come and teach musical rounds and some instrument lessons to the children as well as a woman from Italy who could teach seven different languages and had an infant in arms whom the students not in a specific class would scoop up at the door. We had a former barefoot excommunicated Catholic monk who came to offer Greek and Latin. We had several folks from the medical and academic worlds come through to offer students information in AIDs awareness and STDs, as well as budgeting, history, politics, and other basic issues relating to their lives. We had a local potter who came in and with the students' assistance reclaimed the old chicken coop and turned it into an art studio complete with wheels and kilns; his claim to fame with the children was that he demanded the students toss their first hundred pots back into the clay bin. As a Buddhist monk, it was vital that he share this practice of non-clinging. But now we needed someone full time; which at the academy began with 24-7 and became endless.

We interviewed some folks and landed a winner; a true renaissance man, he was trained as a civil engineer but was so well read and brilliant that he was not limited by it. He played many instruments and had an excellent working knowledge of mathematical principles, Lakota training in sweat lodge and other integral human practices, understood the English language as only a poet etymologist may when not limited to English and could fix a hopeless bus engine in the middle of a highway in the rain without proper tools; he could tolerate living for weeks on end in crowded spaces with needy teenage people, and he could find his way through the deep woods in the dark regardless of proper markers. And perhaps most critically, he was dedicated to his own growth as a human being. I finally had another real adult full time. A quality one. It was this man who made a necessary statement one midday circle when the school was bursting with several dozen students and a variety of teacher people moving through. And I got to watch it all unfold so exquisitely, so beautifully, as he provided some young men an experience I could not ever have provided.

As I said, we were bursting with students that year and had many groups of students involved with myriad studies. There was a group of young bucks in their early teens who had decided to create a little fort in a triangle of trees in the woods near the wetlands, which would have been fine and dandy, except that they opted to use it as a smoking den of stupidity. And that is when he became involved. Unbeknownst to me, he made his way down to their wooded hideout with an old used empty brown lunch sack and gathered up countless cigarette butts from the ground they had desecrated. He returned to midday circle, had his meal quietly, and when it was time for discussion and announcements, he stood, slowly, silently, his precious bag gripped in his hand. And then he began to chant. And rant. And chant. Dancing slow motion style around the circle and then weaving himself through the bodies, he chanted louder and louder. I have no idea what he was saying specifically but I guarantee you he had us all wondering. At this point the young bucks still had no idea he had visited their outpost and harvested their waste, but they discovered that fact quickly. He shook the bag of butts around as a rhythmic accompaniment for about three rounds of the circle, and then, then he stopped in the middle of the circle facing the guys primarily responsible, was silent for a moment, and then, well, gives me shivers to remember it all. He began a howling sort of repertoire, and as he reached into his bag for fistfuls of cigarette butts he danced about the young men wailing them at their heads and bodies as they ducked and hid beneath their hands and arms. When he was out of butts and breath, he stopped just as silently as he had begun, bowed to the students involved and made his way back to his spot in the circle. And that was that. We did not say anything further about it. The point had been made for anyone willing to hear. But after circle, the guys took some garbage bags down to their attempted man-cave and cleaned and deconstructed the whole place.

It was only because the circle was known through and through to be a safe place, a grounded place, and one in which the truth, regardless of how heinous or messy, would be readily available, that such things were possible. I share this example to show as much as possible in a single scene, but we were in circle three times a day, sometimes seven days a week, and I can guarantee that the full, even unimaginable range of possibilities of what was addressed and created and absorbed through that holy vortex has stayed with all of us who shared it in integral ways. The circle was indeed at the center of it all, the hub. But there were an unlimited number of spokes and wheels and efforts that emanated from it and led us to whatever was needed or possible to learn.

We frequently bumped up against societal expectations evidently embedded and standardized within the American educational experience – things such as report cards, dances, sports, celebrations, and, of course, graduation. Given we had a thorough commitment to not act in some automatic way if possible, when any of these expectations were raised, we had to stop and say, wait a minute, what was the original intent of such a thing? And then, if the intention made sense in regard to what the children needed or would benefit from, we'd figure out how we could meet the basic requirement by definition while remaining true to the intent but without forfeiting originality and the possibility of refining or recapturing something within the context of the expectations. So when the first batch of youngsters got to the age or maturity to move on from the academy, we had to stop and consider this whole animal called graduation. Of course, true to form, the first thing to do was to investigate the original meaning of the term. What was this thing we called graduation, and was it of value to us, and if so, what could we design and create to honor it?

For the initial etymological research, we used our default text (though the term default settings had yet to be used in popular speech) – The American Heritage Dictionary. With minimal research, we discovered that the term derived from the Latin word "gradus", which means "to step, such as to step up a ladder or stair;" figuratively, "a step toward something, a degree of something rising by stages". Of course, that was interesting, but we always liked to get as close to the root as we could. It turned out that the original Anglo-Saxon root is "ghredh" – which means simply "to walk" or "to go".

Now this seemed pertinent, for it was time for them to walk on, to go off and discover whatever may be next for them. And so it was a combination of things. It involved more questions, which meant more searching and wondering. Is a student ready to go? How would we know for sure? How could we make sure they were prepared as fully as possible for the mess we knew was waiting out there for them? What was important to know? To be prepared to do? How could we help them determine what was next if they were unclear? Was a ceremony to honor the "graduates" important? If so, what was integral to such a celebration? What about diplomas? We were hardly about handing preprinted papers to students… how could a diploma carry the spirit and intention of the school and the work the students had participated in there? We questioned everything we could in an attempt to be a bit more aware and less automatic, more authentic and less mindless. We wanted nothing to do with mindlessness.

In regard to the whole graduation gig, we already had some things in place, given that we had already been using portfolio assessment for years and had had gazillions of meetings and conversations about what any given individual or group of students needed, daily at a minimum. We had also established by this point a clear understanding of the importance of the blended balance of basic expectations and specific needs when working with any group. So we had some elements from which to draw upon. And of course, it was a process; one that lasted as long as the school did and was tuned with each passing year and each new group of cheery faces readying for the next arena.

We had been slowly accruing a list of graduation requirements for years as we watched and listened and learned about what was needed and what was useful, so it was not difficult to finalize it, as much as we ever finalized anything. We had the usual academic culprits covered – readin', writin', n 'rithmetic. Our overarching aim went as far beyond that as possible for each child; we wanted to prepare the young folks so that when they walked out the school house doors for the last time, they would have every possible option open to them, as well as some self confidence. They needed to read and write and do arithmetic. But they needed to have a grasp on much more than that. In fact, the reading and writing and arithmetic were not the central concern for us – most of our students were far ahead of their peers in public school academically due simply to the attention received.

Self-awareness, awareness of others, respect for self and all other beings including mother earth and all our fellow beings, creativity, service, integrity, these were our primary concerns. Long after the academy closed its doors, I heard of something in public school called "character education". Now there are "community schools" and SEL (social emotional learning). Now it has names. There were many new theories and models named later that I had to stop and say, hm. It now has a name. We thought it was simply called education, learning, becoming human, responsible development. None of the public or private schools I eventually worked in came anywhere close to what we were able to create together at the academy, though I and many other individual teachers certainly did what we could.

As with all else, the graduation requirements at the academy had to reflect who we were as a school, as a group of people striving to become ourselves amidst the mindlessness of the world, and so they were diverse and extensive. All the usual academic state demands were there. In fact, that was the easy part for most. We had students take their college boards when they were ready rather than when they would have in public school. We had students achieve perfect scores two years before their friends in public as well as fancy private schools. But there was much, much more. Students needed to know basic things such as how to diaper a baby, how to change a tire and check oil, how to get to a nyc and back without enough money (legally too, and yes, I needed to say that). They had to complete an internship for at least six weeks in a field of interest. They needed to design and host an art event in a public venue. They had to complete an extensive service project. They had to present their final portfolio of work to parents and friends in a formal presentation. And, quite frankly, they had to put up with me and my constant demands that they reach further or deeper daily for however many years they'd been there.

One of the first things we decided concerned the diplomas. We could satisfy the needs of colleges, universities, and other programs which demanded a paper diploma by simply putting a formal letter stating they met the requirements in their files, which by this time were a vast collection of narrative reports concerning everything from academics to arts to self-awareness. No problem there. (For years afterwards, I received calls and emails from admission officers telling me that the narrative reports were the most amazingly comprehensive and insightful files regarding students that they had ever received. Imagine that. And no grades whatsoever anywhere.)

We decided, as we often did, to let the students decide. They could determine what they wanted the diplomas to be made of, what tangible material or materials would best represent them as a small group of individuals. The first year it was bluestone which I was to carve. But what was I to carve into it? Their names? They knew their names and this was for them, not anyone else. After a few practice swipes carving the stone, I realized I wasn't going to say much at all. Then I saw it; all they needed from me at this point was one last assignment, one last task, one last trait to develop as we set them loose on the world. And so, I only carved a single word in each, a word that would convey their next and probably last assignment from me and other faculty folks; it simply stated their next piece of work on themselves: courage, integrity, humility, lightness, awareness, lovingkindness… you get the idea. In the ensuing years, we had diplomas of stained glass, maple wood recorders, clay lanterns, all with a word somehow integrated into them to convey what each person needed to develop next.

When we finally had a couple of graduation ceremonies under our belts, we had a pretty cool gig going which lasted for days and culminated in a public ceremony under a big tent in the adjoining meadow on the Sunday of Memorial Day weekend for family and friends to enjoy. The actual graduation celebration, so to speak, began far sooner than the public ceremony however. It took about a week at its finest as I recall. At the beginning of the last week of school, we would all bid farewell to the folks leaving (between three and eight people) and one of the teachers and some helpers took them up into the mountains to embark upon a four-day process involving a sweat lodge, a vision quest, another sweat, and plenty of journaling and processing. While the "graduates" were in the mountains, the rest of the students took trips to the salvation army store to obtain white clothes and then cooked piles of food for the folks who would be returning on Friday. They also worked to prepare the school building and grounds for their return as well as for the big event.

When the grads returned, several things occurred either simultaneously or in quick succession. Once we welcomed them back with songs and cheers, we'd gather to share stories and wishes. The students leaving formed a small circle within the larger circle of teachers and younger students, facing out into the larger circle. One by one, the small band of grads shared their stories of sitting out in the woods and all that had transpired for them in the 72 hours they waited and watched, seeking guidance. And one by one, once the vision quest stories were told, one by one, the younger students and teachers would make wishes for them each and all. The younger students and teachers who had stayed behind were already in their white clothing but the folks who had been left out on the rocks for a few days were pretty groatie. Once the stories were told and wishes were made, singing songs and drumming, we walked in procession-like form across the property, down to the stream and across to the rail trail, then off to the right to the waterfall, where we gathered in the gully around the falling water. It was the end of May in upstate New York; the water was as clear and cold as it was abundant coming off the cliffside.

There were many things we did at the school which would not be possible today. This is one of them. Each graduate, one at a time, stripped off their grimy clothing and stepped under the water long enough to let it stream through their hair and down their bodies and allow them to howl a bit. When they stepped out, there were fresh towels and clean white clothes for them to step into. Then we all, still singing and drumming, made our way back to the schoolhouse for the feast.

Since we had been shoeless, our feet were thick with mud when we returned, so I had a hose and bowl and cloth at the entryway and washed everyone's feet as they arrived. And yes, of course it was symbolic, though I honestly at this point cannot say what it symbolized for me. Service of course. Though it was not entirely symbolic. It was also practical. We considered the schoolhouse a sacred space and did not wear street shoes inside; we all had what we called indoor shoes – most of us using the little black cotton shoes you find quite cheaply in Asian outlet stores. Though we would have certainly considered the muddy feet less disrespectful than we would the street dirt from shoes… there was another practical consideration, one that was the impetus to change footwear when entering the schoolhouse for everyone there: dirt. Dirt which needed to be cleaned up at the end of every day and every event. By us. The students and teachers. Cleaning up after ourselves was an ending 15 minute daily practice as well as the focus of monthly family work weekends. There was no janitor to call.

And then, renewed and clothed in white, our feet clean, we gathered in our circle and feasted and sang and drummed and danced and celebrated for hours. It was however, not some mindless party. Everyone served each other food rather than themselves, we shared more stories of what we would remember most from the year, we drummed and chanted and danced; there was more clarity in the room than chaos. The day ended as all days ended, in circle, making announcements and singing a song and hugging good bye, albeit temporarily, as we would all be involved in setting up and making food for the big ceremony scheduled in two days, after which we were all heading out for our annual school end spring camping journey to the national park on the barrier islands the day after that. So no, it never really ended.

The big event didn't last very long. We didn't expect the same degree of patience and interest from friends and families as we did our students in regard to ceremonies in the hot sun, so we kept it short and to the point, affording everyone enough of a taste of who we were that they felt well fed in every way. Given that we had very few folks graduating on any year, (three to nine), and given we had no ranking or grade system, everyone was a valedictorian. Here was an opportunity for each student and teacher to say a few words regarding what they had learned, what they intended and hoped to carry forth into the future or larger world. There were also music, dance, and poetry presentations, and there was always an art show and portfolio presentations throughout the schoolhouse displayed for folks to enjoy after the formal ceremony ended. I will say that folks ate this all up. And not just the incredible, plentiful East Indian food that we'd cooked up either – every song, every story. This was frequently the case whenever we hosted any event. Folks responded with gushing praise and genuine gratitude. Most of America is spiritually starved as we all know, and we were evidently providing some rare and rich fare.

Another public school-like expectation began to be murmured about only about two years into the school: dances. School dances to be precise. One year, there was an explosion of interest in swing dance. We did what we did whenever such an interest arose; we had a basic way of handling anything the students requested to learn. They would need to come up with enough students willing to make the commitment, find a teacher and convince them to work for little or nothing, make the money to pay for whatever would be involved, and schedule it with everything else going on in mind.

Writing this, I am aware of how many different reactions and responses there may to be to this way of operating. I can't say I initially did such a thing so that the children would develop real world skills in everything from budgeting and marketing to navigating personal and social relationships to accomplishing a task to serve something bigger than themselves, though those did occur. I did it initially for two reasons. One, we had no funds available to pay me a livable wage or to buy furniture and supplies for the school let alone extras. Two, I saw no reason why people over the age of 13 or

14 with ideas should require anything more than guidance and assistance in tight spots from the adults around them to realize their goals. They wanted to swing dance, then figure out how to swing dance. It isn't brain chemistry. (Though I myself would be learning that to teach it eventually as well in a thematic study entitled Perception.) The two or three people who had hatched out the request gathered up most of the other students, found an adult with experience who was willing to teach them, and held a regular and rather zesty swing dance class a couple days a week. Ta da.

I am going to stop and pontificate again here, albeit briefly, I hope. Our children are much more capable, bright, and sturdy than most adults like to admit. We continually infantilize them as preparation to fill a proper post in society where they can be told what to do and do it. Sit down and shut up. Do not think for yourself, do not press limits, do not express your true thoughts and feelings, do not imagine for a minute you can achieve your dreams. Oh, I know, I know, there are currently plenty of hip programs with the accompanying jargon available for our children as we slowly begin to swing back and forth between the liberal, more humane side of the pendulum as a society and an insidious racist misogynist force with tentacles throughout all our national services and structures. However, when it comes to our schools, our educational system itself, in reality, despite the best efforts of some students and teachers to create corners and safe places and valuable programs wherein students and teachers work together to create real learning experiences, there is far more of an investment from the system itself in maintaining the status quo. Oftentimes, the demands from the system via administrators act only to hinder and block the exiting possibilities of real learning. I'm betting most teachers reading this may chuckle sadly, or even weep genuinely, at my minimization of the damage done.

Liability and political popularity have become far more important considerations than education, which means growth, which always demands change accompanied by discomfort. There is an old Peanuts' cartoon in which Lucy reminds Schroeder that "no system is going to educate you to overthrow them…" My response? Unless the system is created by and comprised of folks invested instead in the maturity, growth, and evolution of our children, our species, our world. I was. My own discomfort was "of no great consequence" in light of what was at stake. Our students had no "administration" of people collecting huge paychecks for telling them what they needed and deserved, what they could and couldn't do. Our children figured those things out for themselves, daily, hourly. Together.

In regard to the swing dance class, yes, you guessed it: it demanded a formal dance to share all the new moves! As I recall, we were nearing the end of autumn one year and the students started talking about a harvest dance. One of the older students, a young woman whose creativity font was never off, was selected by her schoolmates to lead the effort. What they came up with, no amount of adult input would have imagined. Everyone dressed as their favorite vegetable, and all costumes had been home made out of whatever could be found in closets or purchased at a used clothing store.

The designs and costumes were heart-stoppingly crazy and elegant and outrageous. Velvet and satin eggplant, corny cartoonish cornstalk, some glow-in-the-dark peas without a pod. As the person primarily responsible for it all, I opted to break out of the veggie category and dressed instead as a honeybee. For that was exactly what I did there at every turn. Pollinated ideas and possibilities.

PUBLIC SCHOOL SURVIVAL STORIES.

In North Carolina I learned a great deal about racism, the degree it permeates both the systems and the human lives who depend on such systems to learn and heal and grow. In New York I was suffocated and starved trying to work within a system severely dilapidated and inhuman; treating mortal wounds daily with band aids takes its toll on everyone involved. On the Texas/Mexico border, I learned about the intense struggle between those willing to risk everything for an education and those who would dismiss them before they could get across the brisge. Following are the stories through which my students in three very different places taught me about what truly matters in the larger world and how being true to themselves in an inhumane system impacted them on a daily, and sometimes eternal, basis.

> "It is only with the heart
> that one sees clearly;
> what is essential
> is invisible to the eye."
> - Antoine de Ste. Exupery

BELOW THE MASON-DIXON LINE

Upon moving into my little rental house in a small, primarily African American working-class neighborhood, my neighbor across the street sent her granddaughter Precious over to ask, no, tell me, to come by. I walked over with Precious and my old hound dawg Jake. Big Momma, as she was known throughout the neighborhood, was ensconced in her double bed in the only bedroom in the small house, well air conditioned and layered in several of those pre-printed velvety plastic blankets you get at Walmart for ten bucks. She patted what little was left of her bedside for me to have a sit. Her youngest charge, Junior, was propped up in bed next to her on the other side, as tiny and frail as she was grand and certain.

"Well, aren't you a sweet one to take time to come on over to see a sick old lady?" she cooed.

I smiled. She wasn't much older than I was at that time. She took one of my hands slowly into hers and patted it.

"I want you to listen to me now," she said almost apologetically but clearly. "Now I ain't no racist, and neither are my grandbabies here." She stopped to twirl her youngest charge's mop of curls and nod to Precious. Satisfied with their silent approval, she continued. "Now if you have any trouble in the neighborhood, any trouble at all, anyone so much as cross their eyes at you or that hound dawg of your'n and you just let me know and I'll make sure you don't have no more trouble after that."

Nothing about her made me doubt that should I have "trouble" she'd find a way to rectify it. But I was a tad shocked by her statement. Something about a huge bed ridden black woman wanting to dispel any notions I had in regard to neighborhood prejudice made me pause mightily. Honestly, I had no idea black folks would ever consider themselves racist; over the years I had lived with and helped to raise young folks of African American descent, and I had never heard anyone ever act like or refer to themselves as racist. Therefore, not the opposite either? I became friendly in that neighborly way with Precious as intermediary; big momma sent me proper North Carolina Sunday dinners she hobbled into her kitchen to make for the whole family and I of course reciprocated with zucchini breads and birthday gifts, attending the celebratory barbecues and taking

Precious along in the car to shop when I went to the grocery store.

When I left the academy, I'd no clue anyone would want me in public schools. I had never been wanted in public schools; why would it be any different as a teacher than a student? But I had borrowed from everyone I knew to keep the school open and it was time to pay the many pipers, which meant working for "the man", for money.

I couldn't stay in New York State to teach as my provisional teaching license had lapsed and in New York, without my master's degree, I couldn't remedy that. In New York, once a person obtains their provisional teaching license, they have ten years in which to earn the masters' degree. If they fail to do so, the provisional license expires and you can't keep teaching without it. I had used up my ten years keeping the academy going. It had permanent certification; I did not.

I looked south, primarily North Carolina, as I had never liked being in a cold, dark environment. I applied for 23 different positions and was offered every single job I applied for. All 23 of them. Over the phone. Sight unseen. But I needed to see. So I took my Jake dawg and we journeyed south to western and then eastern North Carolina to see what we could see and do some interviewing. Ultimately, we landed in the great dismal swamp, a beautiful place despite its name, a land of cabbage and potato farms snuggled amidst the ocean sounds. It was here my real public education actually began.

I took the position because it was the right mix of curriculum creation, counseling, and teaching and the folks seemed good hearted. I tried to set aside my own bias against racists. I would be working in a small county district 50% of the time as the gifted services coordinator and 50% as an Honors English teacher in the one and only high school in the county. Though told I'd be coordinating gifted services for all three of the schools in the district - elementary, middle, and high - it's not exactly what occurred. Here was my first taste of official public-school politics adult-style. The special services director, who the position of gifted services coordinator fell under, already had a person working at the elementary school who was quite identified with her post and not at all interested in working with anyone else. She had lived there forever and her husband was the Baptist minister, which was akin to mayor in more northerly climes; perhaps the director didn't like conflict. Despite all my efforts to clarify the position, I was only ever met with either an absurd sort of blank stare, or a falsely sympathetic nod of agreement. But no clarifications. There are gazillions of people in administrative positions who are spineless liars, but I don't suppose that surprises anyone. It's quite obvious, given how much we celebrate when folks aren't like that. Be nice if that ratio was different, but it isn't.

I, a strange white woman, would have been bad enough, but I was a yankee, or a damn yankee according to some, and I was also he worst kind of yankee, a New Yorker. Suspicious to the core. But despite my strange origins I was embraced by almost everyone there; those who were wary didn't let it show due to southern hospitality edicts. However, there was only one woman who befriended me in any real way in the two years I was there. Edicts have their limitations… saying hello and smiling is enough.

My "office" didn't exist, nor any room of any sort where I could keep my things or get organized, let alone meet with students and parents. When I asked about a place from which to operate, I was told one thing by the principal, another by the librarian, yet another by the custodian. It didn't help that the building was undergoing major construction expansion. I ended up commandeering a corner of the library much to the librarian's open chagrin. I staked my claim and tried to figure out what to do. I had no supervisor and no one had held the position previously as it was a newly created position; so, no paperwork, no guidelines, nada. Fortunately, I knew the only thing that mattered were the youngins. And I knew they'd help me figure it out. And they did.

As "gifted services coordinator" I was responsible for coordinating services for students who'd been categorized as "gifted", so I set about to discover who these folks were, and to set up some meetings for them in groups in the library so I could meet them en masse. It was a starting point. And here was one of the first things I discovered: though the school district and county were 50% Caucasian and 50% African American demographically, there were very, very few black students designated as gifted. Not cool. Not cool at all. I had many students, black and white, in my two honors English classes, and what this meant was that some of the brightest, most imaginative and mature minds in the school weren't receiving any services at all simply because their skin was dark. My inner moral compass was screaming in circular alarm. And so, the first thing I did was upset the apple cart by changing up the determination process effective immediately so that the blatant racism would be not be able to continue as readily, perhaps. At least in the gifted services realm while I was there.

Fortunately, as a facet of the gig, the district picked up the tab for me to attend classes held locally by UNC staff and earn state certification in gifted education, K through 12. The certification, which I did earn in the two years allotted, was a whole other educational wake up call. I have several vivid memories of this training – but the most vivid happened early on – we'd gotten an introduction to the course, and with it came several handouts. One was a list of characteristics common to a gifted child. I was shocked. It was a description of me! These were my thought processes, my capacities. And then there was an accompanying list of behaviors which came along and were especially problematic in an American school system whose rote learning sans creative outlets had spelled early death for me and many others I'd encountered along the way. No creative outlets in the classroom, no chance to go ahead of the class with reading … I flashed back to how many times I'd been kicked out of a classroom because we'd been reading as a class and I'd finished the chapter before the others were done with page one. Boredom is not a productive thing; an idle creative mind can and has done much damage in every classroom in this country. When we got out of the training that day, I phoned my sister-mum halfway across the world.

"You're not going to believe this!" I yelled through the phone to her in Nanjing, China, "but it I think I'm gifted!"

There was rich laughter on the other end of the line.

"No shit," she chuckled.

It must have been through this coursework that I discovered some resources to help me figure out how to approach the racist guidelines that promoted white students hundreds of times more often than their black friends. The fact that many of the white students labeled as gifted only had their daddy's last name and momma's whole-hearted righteousness to slide them onto that list did not escape my notice. I knew from having them inappropriately placed in my honor's English classes. There could be no other reason they'd been designated other than politics. They were the children of the school board members and some of the teachers and the wealthiest farmers. It was their system – they built it (or was it their slaves, the grandparents of the black students unconsidered who shared the same last names with the white offspring?) – and by gum they were gonna come first. Now here's a racist statement for you from me: black folks rarely if ever have entitlement issues. It is actually comic (if it weren't so tragic) for white folks to call black folks "entitled", especially since this is usually what is said when what is being requested is far less than what is way past due.

Anyhoo, I discovered an IQ test, standardized no less, which had been created specifically to afford rural African American students a fair shake – simply by utilizing questions and terminology derived from their own cultural and personal world, rather than a world they had never even been invited into. Imagine that. Now it became immediately possible for our black students to sit for this exam in place of the standard "white" exam and ensured it could be used to determine a student's IQ should it be warranted. I encountered this same culturally/geographically testing language everywhere I went in the public school systems. It is no wonder to me why the white rises to the top in this nation; every system, down to its most minute, seemingly unimportant specifics, was created exactly so that the white could rise to the top.

I also instituted a selection process for gifted services that demanded a student meet five out of eight determining factors rather than simply the IQ test, other standardized exams, or class grades. I added sections which catered to other characteristics of gifted individuals, including creativity and leadership and mechanical abilities, which opened things up for the musical and artistic geniuses, as well as those with mechanical prowess.

I had discovered what I suppose I had always known from my own experiences already, the folks who were there to educate others, who were not often gifted themselves, had some strange ideas about genius. It was white and well-mannered, like their Jesus. But it certainly didn't describe any genius I'd ever met.

I don't honestly know how this was all received because, as we all know, folks lie and pretend more often than speak their truth. On top of that was a layer of ice simply because I was an outsider. Southern hospitality edicts demand a welcoming posture, but no need to cozy up to strangers.

Especially from a place as wanton as New York, which to everyone outside of the northeast United States, means New York City. Somehow, no one in the larger nation remembers that the state is hundreds of times the size of the city, with millions of people and quite a range of demographics. At any rate, no one bothered to do much more than say hello for some months; waiting and watching as it were. I spent time getting to know the students and figuring out how I could best serve them. I knew from the academy experience that what I referred to as a "missionary style" relationship, rather than useful, was potentially harmful. What this means is simple really, don't offer someone something you think they need or want in order to improve their quality of life before you ask for gawd's sake. Ask what is needed, then work together to create it, learn from each other. Do not assume your needs are theirs. Do not assume you know what is needed. Just ask. Watch. Respond. Grow.

Once I started to become more educated about gifted services in public education, I sought out ways in which I could share the information and possibilities with my fellow educators. Most "gifted services programs" in this country, when they do exist, exist as just that, programmed. They are not organic structures, growing out of genuine needs, watered with real possibilities for exploration. This new way of offering more fluid and useful services within an archaic system required that I go find individual teachers who may be open to doing things a little differently. I would ask them if I could visit them in their classroom and make an appointment if they said yes. I'd ask them what they were teaching, what students were learning; I'd look at some student work, ask what was most frustrating. Lots of questions. But my questions were born from a genuine interest and wish to learn, and so the need to become defensive rarely arose. It was a perilous balance, one I had learned how to maintain from my time with the academy community.

One of the teachers who decided to give it a whirl was definitely unexpected. I hadn't even been invited into her classroom yet. An upper level mathematics teacher with a reputation as a serious hard ass, I'm not sure I ever saw the woman smile. She came to me one morning in the library before the bell rang and got right to the point.

"I have eight youngins in my trig class who already understand what we're studying and another 30 who are completely lost," she came right to the point.

"Okay," I said shrugging and looking her in the eye. Eight math geeks; no problem.

I smiled inside; trigonometry no less. Something else I was completely clueless about but was supposed to teach? But that wasn't a problem, given what the folks at the academy had taught me. I knew that a teacher didn't need to have any specific information to teach; I simply needed to be willing to learn enough to guide them through designing and implementing a project that would allow them to cement their learning through a creative effort together. Teachers don't need to know anything other than how to learn. That's what we really impart or fail to impart when we teach. For me, teaching is more about blindly leading the sighted into places that demand they close their eyes and reach for each other's hands, move toward a deeper understanding within themselves, in the context of their own life. Then open their eyes and live accordingly.

"Well," she wanted to know, "How does this work?"

"When do you have them?" I asked.

"Eighth period," she said.

I shrugged again. "Send them over," I suggested. "We'll figure out a project for them to show what they know."

I don't believe we truly learn something until we use that knowledge to create something new or fresh with it. Or with the questions that rise out of the knowledge attained. Creative educational ventures often yield questions asked and unasked, known and unknown. We've replaced this genuine knowledge in the US with measuring how well someone can vomit rote facts. A tragedy. Also one. if not the primary reason, we are far down on the rating list educationally among other "developed" countries.

I already knew the students fairly well; they were in my honor's English class as well as on the growing list of "gifted" students warranting services. We met later that day as I recall; they strolled into the library right after the Pavlovian bell ring, excited, aloof, wary, curious, the whole gamut. They plunked themselves down at one of the big wooden library tables and assumed their positions, you know, the ones we've all donned by the age of 14 as full body and facial armor to keep ourselves safe out there in teen-ville. These were the "cream of the crop", as some of the teachers and administrators referred to them, but there was only one single person among them with any sense of awareness and presence. Presence and awareness are rarely taught or conveyed in public education, other than using tools in a shop class or yoga in phys ed. Sadly, presence and awareness demand a consistent presentation; these are not learned in a class with a test, or in any class at all for that matter. These qualities must be seen in the lives of the adults around them if they are to be taught for real. The students who shine like beacons for others are true to themselves and compassionate with others as much as possible, even in the public high school arena. I had met this young man's folks; they also had a penchant for looking a person in the eye, practicing kindness and compassion, demanding respect by respecting others - not common qualities in my experience, but ones which can certainly be passed on via both nature and nurture. Being present and aware was valued and taught at home, allowing him to share such things with his fellow learners. Extremely rare. Plato would have been proud?

When a group of learners contains one person with natural presence, just one who has resisted donning the cloaks of the ignorant dramas which serve as prevalent defense mechanisms in our young people's world, it allows things to happen that otherwise wouldn't occur, and with a fraction of the effort on the teacher's part. A natural leader, which is what these folks often become in the larger world if they survive the system, for they are not ever followers of anything but their own questions and longings, works to inspire and coalesce fellow students with such ease that I, as a teacher, often simply stand back and offer help; it becomes more a matter of watching something amazing unfold than it is leading anyone anywhere. Without such a beacon in a group, the teacher must hand-feed the students' questions and creative ideas. It's akin to starting a campfire in the rain. With one person wide awake, the fire sparks and grows. Astonishingly quickly. And I become a mere fire tender.

I make an effort not to begin anything without pausing enough to get everyone quiet, and despite everyone telling me it was impossible to do so in a public school setting, I recited a poem or sang a song with students together each time before starting a class or journey. Some of them learned and memorized each word and inflection as it was fed to them. Memorization and recitation are lost arts. Aside from all the intellectual and academic attributes they inspire, such a practice clears the air, and gets everyone in the same room at the same time in a matter of moments.

"Welcome everyone," I said very quietly to those listening, immediately catching the attention of some of the more attention-seeking drama queens, who quieted rather than miss anything. And of course, being southern stock youngins with "home trainin' ", they shooshed each other and looked up to meet my gaze.

"What poem?" I asked, as they had by now memorized a decent number of poems and songs to choose from. Someone suggested we do "The Jabberwocky", as I had recently let them know its author was a genius mathematician. We stood together in a small circle around the table and recited the piece in a lively enough manner to warrant the librarian's glare. Ah well.

"Okay," I said once everyone sat back down. "How much do you know about why you're here?"

This is always the first thing to establish – knowns and unknowns. Establishing common understanding is a step all too often forgotten in an attempt to achieve something haphazardly in a given amount of time. It requires some time and effort but without it, there is no basic understanding from which to move as a group and so it is doomed to be a sporadic effort led by the same people all the time.

It's a common thread throughout learning in schools, all grades, ages, levels, studies – in a group, the same people do all the work, every time. It's why serious learners and creators feel encumbered by group work; it isn't group work – it's the most responsible, creative, and organized people being made responsible for several other students on top of their own work. I'm sure this rings true for many folks out there.

I was greeted with the usual range of responses.

"She's sick of us," someone offered, overlapped by laughter and several other responses. "We're a pain in the butt," "We're going to bake cookies?", "We're here to save humanity!" and so on.

"Okay," I summarized, no emotion, trying to maintain my focus on wha was true. "Now, using what you know is true, what do you think? Your teacher isn't particularly prone to tossing you out because she's sick of you. You went from being bored in a trig class to a meeting with me as your mentor for gifted services in the library. What could it be?"

They had no clue. Seriously. Not a one. At least no one was going to risk it.

"Tell us," they cried out, not being students who have much experience and therefore no tolerance with "not getting it" immediately.

This entire group of kiddos sought to grab onto information and hold it high before another as though some sort of an award or validation perhaps. It's who they believed they were, it's what was expected, what they did; it's why they were valuable to their family members and teachers. Clueless regarding intrinsic value, every raised hand was a claim not necessarily for fame, but it was a simple, now-ingrained, effort to further cement their value within their peers eyes as well as the system itself.

"You tell me first," I sat down at the table with them with a notebook and pen and suggested they may wanna take notes too. They immediately scrambled for their backpacks and rifled through to get what they needed. Some of course, sought more exact instructions.

"What should we put the notes in? Pen or pencil, miss?" and then the constant question I faced here, "Is this gonna be graded?" I took a deep breath.

"None of this is graded," I said. "I'm not here to grade; I'm here to learn as much as I can." I will admit that I was always more a philosophy teacher than anything else. "You're all here because you understand what your class is studying and your teacher said you were bored," I looked around to see the responses – quizzical, concerned, fearful even, some interest, a couple of lights. "So, tell me, what exactly do you understand about what she's teaching right now?"

Of course, one must always be prepared for the most literal of brilliant students. "We aren't there in her class right now," someone offered, only half in jest, "We don't know what she's teaching." Thankfully, he was checked by his neighbor's disgusted moans and I didn't need to respond. I'm not sure I would have anyway, as I prefer to focus on what is possible, rather than what is pulling attention away from what is possible. My silence and open gaze, pen poised over my own journal, inspired them to continue in a more fruitful vein.

All too often, teachers and parents move to fill the empty spaces of not knowing in an effort to comfort and control. We all know that when we fill an empty space, no one else can. I was primarily there for them, not me, and so my discomfort at silent, empty places was of no consequence. I wasn't there to fill them; in fact, I was there to create the spaces, allow them, and to teach the young people how to do the same thing. So that when they don't know something in life, rather than rushing to fill the void with ignorance and fancy, and then waste a lifetime of energy defending it all as precious, they'll have the ability to sit and wait and investigate and listen and then, perhaps, better understand the actual information when it is revealed. Better understand what to do with it. Children need to learn how to milk those empty quiet places, to see what is there before throwing something in just because it looks like it could fit. To sit with possibilities and watch for what they may become prior to investing themselves in a specific effort. To learn how not to know, peacefully, and to know only that that is the point from which we can learn.

Given how lost they were at this point, I suggested they all write down everything they could in the next three minutes about what they were learning in the trig class as specifically as possible. Now they could focus individually on what they knew and getting it down on paper as fast as possible. They knew this game better, though of course some sought further specifics and parameters. I refused with my silence, looked at the clock to let them know time had started. That got them, and within seconds everyone was scrambling to write down everything they knew about coordinate systems in trigonometry. It is possible to turn one's worst learned behaviors in a way that they can be used to their own benefit.

"Okay," I announced when I noticed the clock, "Times up. Who wants to read first? And make sure you take notes so everyone has the cumulative knowledge."

These being well-mannered youngins, hands were raised.

"Just go ahead and read when you're ready," I reminded them. "Try to be aware enough of each other that you don't need permission to speak."

They looked around at each other, afforded the usual herd glances and hints to each other. Pecking orders are not just for chickens or pigeons. I was continually amazed at how few skills teenage people had available in regard to presence, awareness, attention, integrity. Scary really. But these are not valued by our society, unless they make someone big money. And so why would we teach them to our children? Why would they ever emulate them? Who could they emulate?

One by one they read, some more general and pondering, some more specific, some with formulas. I simply kept reminding them to fill in what classmates were adding to their own lists so that everyone could get it all down; I urged questions or clarifications. The library where we were meeting wasn't actually called a library anymore, having been re-designated a media center and now boasting rows of shiny new computers. They caught my eye as I listened to them read. Here was something I hadn't had as a tool or resource previously; here was something these students were all too familiar with as they were growing up alongside the growing computer and internet era. When the last person finished, I suggested they go as a pack over to the computers and find a project on the internet that they could design and implement together – something real – something that would use as much of what they had written down as possible in the real world outside. I went back to some other work; they were off and running.

The next day, they presented their plan. They were going to create a sundial, but not just any sundial, a sundial for the elementary school playground that used the human form standing in the middle as its gnomon. Nicely done. My role became purely advisory. In a small town setting like this, these students had been in the same learning groups since childhood, except that now there were more black faces included in the circle due to my having changed the parameters. But this wasn't problematic to any of them; they'd been playing sports and picking crops together for years. Generations in fact. I helped with making lists and securing materials, tools, permissions for this and that. Every day for about a week, rather than go to trig, they'd report in to me, make an intention for the day, and get to work. Near the end of the project, we headed up to the elementary school playground for some minor construction. Within a few days, they had created something they hadn't even known was possible a couple of weeks ago; they had further coalesced as a creative, collaborative group of learners; and they had gifted the younger children and elementary teachers with a new instructional playground toy. They also earned the administrators another feather in their proverbial caps.

We held an opening ceremony one Saturday afternoon, cut a ribbon, and served refreshments. I like to follow through with things clearly until they end, and I believe in ceremonies and rituals as a way to both signify and celebrate a culmination of an effort made. Of course, my original ceremony only included classmates and parents, but the principal saw a political opportunity and ran with it. The one county newspaper was there, board members, etc. I stepped back, let the students talk it up, left early, quietly. There is always a danger that a teacher be mistaken for the wonder they cultivate in the children; I never wanted any of that at the academy when folks started to mistake me for the amazing progress their child was making, and I wanted no part of it here. My job was to make sure they got a copy of the newspaper story for their personal files as such things would be handy when most would likely be applying for university in a couple of years.

After some months of waiting each other out and observing, there were a couple of folks who managed to reach out. One was a parent of a truly gifted student of mine. The parent was a tortured soul who was no doubt gifted himself; he knew well that regardless of any services his kids needed to get out of the county if they were ever going to become themselves fully. Better yet, the state. He, his wife, and many children adopted me as an aunty figure for the duration of my stay and honestly, I'm not sure I would have made it two years without their warmth and generosity, the family dinners and country drives.

The other person I ended up working closely with taught me tremendous lessons about southern etiquette, racism, fortitude, integrity, grit, and so much more. We met because she held one of the four most critical posts in any high school – she was the main office lady, and she was about as no muss, no fuss as they make us humans. She was not to be confused with the other person in the office, another one of the top four, the principal's secretary. In fact, you'd not want to ever confuse these two; they despised each other quite openly.

The main office lady is a supreme post, in caps. She may not be the principal's secretary but this one had his ear between her fingers and he listened carefully to her because he knew she knew everything, absolutely everything, that was going on and around school property and beyond. She pulled no punches either; while his secretary was a bit of a kiss ass, she was not. He'd walk past and she's stage whisper fiercely to him, "straighten yer tie!" Then she'd look at me, make a prissed up face and say something like, "no home trainin'," quite sincerely and disgustedly.

My dear friend was of old southern stock, but not ignorant of today's world by any stretch. She was an Episcopalian, and that made a difference there, where your faith represented far more than a song list on Sundays. The fact that she was not Baptist, or at the very least Methodist, connoted that she was more accepting of alternate lifestyles, more than likely even a gawddammed liberal, and in her case it was true. She somehow knew I was not your standard heterosexual woman and let me know, just enough and discreetly enough, that it made no never mind to her who people loved, who they were in their private life. Their life, their business. She also insisted she was not a racist, and it was true that despite most folks sitting in circles of their own skin color at faculty meetings or other school gatherings, she often sat with her lifetime friend, an African American woman who was the business education instructor. She was actually so open and above board with who she was and what she believed that I felt quite comfortable asking her the more uncomfortable questions. Once, her friend had gotten some bad news and was wailing quite sadly in the hallway en route to her classroom while we were working in an adjacent room with the door wide open. She looked over at me.

"Black folks are so emotional," she said matter-of-factly. There was no judgement or negativity in her tone, per se. Still, I was somewhat taken aback; I asked her what she meant. This is always a safe question when asked with the correct tone – the one where the only reason you're asking it is because you genuinely wish to understand something.

"I *mean*," she said emphasizing "mean". "Black folks are more emotional – men and women – it's their culture," Then, after seeing my expression and as though she had just thought of an excellent teaching example, she added, "What? It's not a racist thing. Just go pray with them in one of their churches sometime."

I smiled wanly, wanting to understand so badly.

"Look," she said as though to a five-year-old, "Us white folks? We aren't allowed to go on like that – we'd get tanned right good now, wouldn't we?"

I muttered something lame about needing to think about all of this.

"We're more **reee-presssss-eeeeed**," she got into my face and drawled slowly, carefully enunciating each syllable of the word repressed, as though it were three instead of two syllables long. She continued, reaching back into the file box in front of her, getting back to work. "Hey," she allowed. "There's calling things true, true, then there's using them agin' other people. Those are two mighty different things."

Her husband was another ball of string. One of those true jovial southern gentlemen you'd love to laugh with but there was this racist hatred so deep and strong that just to go near him was too painful. It wasn't as though anyone really conversed around him though; he didn't leave much room for that. His people had been farmers but he and his sons had sold most of it off and invested in a hauling company. They spent most of their time in their huge rigs now, hauling stone and sand sometimes hundreds or even thousands of miles.

But my friend, she hauled her own ass all day. That's what I know. Despite the technology available to phone a teacher or student in a given classroom, she preferred to deliver notes in person. Everywhere, all day long; she loved to walk the halls briskly, and she rarely stopped to chat. That just wasn't what she was here for. She was truly an unwavering soul. She arrived early and left on time and never stopped the entire time. I never knew her to take a break of any sort, ever. She was there to do a job and she was gonna do it fully. And no one could say she didn't.

The office lady is probably the most critical post in the school though some would claim it's really the head custodian. I don't hedge bets; if I have a new position in a new school, you better believe I come bearing gifts whenever possible. This is a critical lesson to any teacher or staff person heading into the public school system. Everything you need is going to have to come through one of these two people, sometimes both. Find out what the office lady and the head custodian like and make sure you keep them happy all year long. Some would call this bribery. I think of it more as tipping. They get the worst of the work, without them the school would fall apart fairly quickly, and they get little to no recognition by society. I won't even go into how pathetic their pay is.. So yeah, I greased the wheel. And I loved it; I absolutely loved bringing something in for someone who never expected it, because not many folks thought of them as anything but work horses who were there solely to attend to their and their students' needs so they could do the more important work of teaching.

Not so fast.

What folks forget is how often it is a person on the support staff in any given school weaves a mentor or guardian like relationship with a student, often a student whom no one else has been able to reach. This includes nurses, bus drivers, teaching assistants, janitors, office ladies, librarians, cafeteria ladies, crossing guards, and on and on. For me, it was the elementary school librarian. I'm not entirely sure I would have made it without her and the option to disappear into the stack of books for hours at a time while the teacher and other students went merrily along within the classroom walls.

My personal experience with formal schooling as a child had cultivated certain ideas about myself as well as many about formal systems. I was too weird, and they had no desire to tolerate the likes of me. These ideas hadn't weakened in the years since childhood. My experiences working with others who had been eaten up and spit out by the system had simply served to harden such notions into facts in my mind. So, when I was called to the principal's office one morning in late autumn, I walked there already planning in my head what I would do after I was fired. Certainly, I would be fired. They'd discovered I was a farce, a fake; I was wrong and broken and not at all what any formal system would wish to tolerate. When I arrived, I was ushered immediately into the principal's office. It didn't help that due to my status of outsider I frequently elicited this painful sort of smile from folks, which is what ushered me through, a series of painful smiles.

An old jock, the principal had a large case of the school athletic trophies in a glass enclosed case lining one wall. We were interrupted by "coach" before we got started; "coach" is the designation one receives in a school district after years of proving oneself as the boys' football/basketball/track coach (girls are less important in our society, and therefore girls' and women's coaches rarely reach the notoriety and respect their male counterparts receive, nor the economic equivalent) sometimes whilst teaching courses full time. It is akin to being designated a living patron saint. As proof, coach had just interrupted a meeting without any warning and our meeting was immediately put on hold when he entered. Ya don't keep gawd waiting.

I sat down. The principal was happy which threw me off. I sat, confused, waiting, uncertain. He conversed intensely with coach about something and had a seat in his fancy black office chair behind his rather ornate wooden desk. When I looked up to try to gauge how bad it was, he was smiling back at me. Beaming even. He pushed a piece of paper across the desk toward me and sat back to beam further. I reached for the paper and read tentatively at first, then, confused, more uncertain, as though perhaps I had stepped into an alternate universe? I read the paper, then looked up to his face to read what was there. What matched? Not my uncertainty, that was sure. The paper had told me I was to receive an award certificate from the school board for outstanding service. It was evidently a big deal in a small district. It's only benefit, which I didn't necessarily see as beneficial, was to appear before the school board all gussied up and listen to them say nice things to me about me without running screaming from the room, receive a useless piece of paper, say nice gratuitous things back to them, then leave. Not my cup of tea. I would have been happy to keep operating quietly, just the kids and their old hippy teacher, under the radar. This on the radar thing was very, very new to me, and I didn't trust any of it as far as I could spit. But I quickly learned the benefit of being on the radar – and it was a benefit that the students could realize immediately, for I discovered we could now essentially do whatever we wanted. Within reason of course.

And this is when I also learned of my added value to the administration and the return for the students. I made the administration look good, and I wanted no credit. In fact, I would have preferred to be ignored completely; attention from the authorities was not something I had been wired for. This meant therefore that my superior officers, which is how I referred to them for no good reason, got all the credit. Which they loved. Absolutely loved. Lapped it up like thirsty dawgs I tell you. I had discovered the ease with which one may maneuver through an ego driven world if one was more than happy to check one's own. And if one isn't concerned with acquiring anything as far as money or awards or credit, it means whomever you are really working for – the children, the mentally ill, the elders, the immigrants – they win, they benefit. There's a very immediately obvious economy to it all. A simplicity and purity that cuts through all the fluff and fat in any system.

One day late in the year I walked into the teacher's lunch room to nab my lunch from the fridge. Coach had a question for me before I could escape. "What I wanna know," he announced rather loudly, "is whether yer a yankee or a damned yankee?"

I wasn't sure. I asked him what the difference was.

"A yankee visits," he replied, looking around the table at his fellow southerners almost conspiratorially, then he looked up at me, his steely blues meeting mine and smoking, and he clarified. "A damn yankee stays."

"I'll keep you posted," was all I said as I smiled at him, turned and left.

I hadn't missed the fact that everyone else in the room had fallen silent waiting for my response. Another litmus test I wondered if I had passed. Though they may have thought I was uncertain whether I was staying or leaving because of my own leanings, I wasn't sure I would be asked to return. Why would I? When one has been deleted and expelled and ditched time and again, year after year, and at very young and therefore impressionable age, one does not extend a hand in trust just because of a couple of experiences that don't fit. It takes much, much more than that.

But perhaps I'm not sufficiently describing myself, and how strange I really was in such an environment. One day, I was in the teacher's room for some reason. Perhaps it was raining, a rare occurrence and one that sent all of us who usually spent most of our time outside, inside. Who knows? I do recall that I was there with our science teacher Mr. Timmy as he was known, and we had been having a brief discussion about his lunch, which was evidently chitlins, and his health – he weighed in at well over 300 pounds. I liked Mr. Timmy, and it seemed mutual. When one of the iguana's in his science classroom finally bit the dust, the students requested I play minister for the funeral. He was happy to have me along. We had a whole funeral procession with songs and a very serious burial replete with more songs out behind the crepe myrtle bushes and I have to say, Mr. Timmy could have put many a Baptist choir to shame for how emotionally he could belt Amazing Grace – all twelve verses mind you. Well, it was a rainy day this day and I was in what was called the teachers' lounge with Mr. Timmy and he had opened his chitlins and started becoming one with them. Not recognizing the substance he was devouring, I asked him what he was eating for lunch.

"Chitlins," he said, and then, reaching into the cooler he brought to school each day, he pulled out more old, greasy plastic containers, plopping them one by one in front of him on the table and continued. "Barbecue, taters, some little piggy feet…" he looked up, smiling, and shrugged, "you know, the usual."

"That shit's gonna kill you ya know, Mr Timmy?"

Somethin's gonna kill me, that's fer sure. Cause we're all of us gonna die." He smiled more broadly. "At least I know what's gonna git me, and at least I'll die smilin'!" He took an extra big spoonful of chitlins and jammed it into his mouth for emphasis. "Mmmmmmmmmmmmmmmmmmm," he said, thinking he was taunting my yankee self.

I had to laugh. True that.

When I went to leave the room, someone had left a big box blocking my path. I stepped onto one of the cushioned chairs and I have no idea why, perhaps thrown back in time by the sensation of stepping onto furniture that wasn't supposed to be stepped upon… but I started hopping from one chair to the next, as though the floor had suddenly become inhabited by the gators who lived quite well in the swamp not far from the school. Mr. Timmy did nothing to dissuade me.

"Now what the hell are you doin?" he demanded, laughing.

"I don't know," I responded at first. Then, "I'm pretending there are gators everywhere and I'm steering clear. Didn't you ever do that as a kid?"

"I woulda got my ass whooped if I had," he said, shaking his head and laughing.

"Well," I countered, "it's not unlike the chitlins though really."

"'What the fuck you talkin' about?"

"Well, you got yer ass whooped anyhow didn't ya?"

He had to laugh, as did I. But before I could get out of the room, Ms. Ellie had arrived with her sack lunch. She stood in the doorway watching and listening. When I saw her, I smiled and shrugged.

"I don't know where you came from," she said grinning, "but boy do we need you here."

And indeed, she probably meant it. Ms. Ellie was a very cool lady – an English teacher, renowned for having absorbed children with nowhere else to go into her household until they could graduate. But unlike the children she absorbed long enough to perhaps change their minds about some of their central personal beliefs regarding themselves, my deepest held beliefs about myself had certainly not yet changed, and so, as with all such statements, it was immediately disregarded, devalued, and discarded like trash. I still saw myself within a world where to trust another person's statements as genuine was considered naïve, at best.

But then it was suddenly springtime and I was asked to return, and having no other clear options, enjoying my time in the sunshine running and cycling along the outer banks' many trails, I signed on for another year at the same position. However, the position I signed on for morphed into something else before we were a month into the school year. By October the one and only guidance counselor at the high school left suddenly when she got a better offer, and I was called upon by the principal to fill her post. I initially resisted. I had and still have a thing about keeping my word, and when I signed the contract with the district, for me, it meant I had given my word to the children that I would be there as their teacher and creative mentor. He begged. He actually begged. And then we concocted some crazy scheme wherein they would hire a couple of other part time folks to serve the designated gifted students and all I had to do was meet with them and guide them. His argument that I may be much more useful to many more students in their critical high school years as a guidance counselor rang true enough to make me stop and consider. Still, it was going to be a phenomenal amount of work with no additional compensation offered other than their need to pay for me to complete a graduate degree in school counseling. So I named my own price.

"I'll do it if you let me have Ms. Betty Jane as the guidance secretary," I said.

"But we've never had a guidance secretary," he claimed, feigning confusion.

"Well," I said from a part of myself I was entirely unfamiliar with, "You're going to have one if you want me as guidance counselor and coordinator of services."

He sighed deeply, not wanting to lose his Betty Jane from the main office, not wanting to deal with the board regarding personnel issues, not wanting to do anything uncomfortable… "How do you know she wants to leave the main office?" he countered.

"We can ask her," I suggested, shrugging. "But I'd put money on it if I had any."

He didn't want to ask her. He didn't want to lose the dynamo who kept the school together for him. But the parents and school board members were all over him about no guidance counselor, and also evidently about me specifically filling the post. So he simply sighed. The way he saw it, he was going to lose no matter what. The way I saw it, I didn't care who lost as long as the students and Ms Betty Jane who had been serving them forever won something.

And so Ms Betty Jane, who was ecstatic to get away from the main office and the personalities at play there, won. But mostly, the students won, for Ms. Betty Jane was an indomitable force, fully committed to the children and their needs. I was off to filling yet another professional position without any preparation, experience, or proper licensure. And once again it seemed to matter less than one may think, for working with youngsters really only requires a deep and abiding care for them and their efforts coupled with a willingness to learn whatever may be needed next.

But neither Ms. Betty Jane nor I could have anticipated what exactly we would be stepping into until we stepped through the guidance office door and realized that no one had filed anything for years. Well, to be completely honest, and remember this was pre-computerized files, there were many files tossed willy nilly into a couple of three and four drawer old metal filing cabinets. All paper. No order we could conceive of ourselves. It may have been considered filed by whomever had been there previously.

This was October; the month when it is already a bit late to get moving on college plans if that is the way a student decided they were heading into the following year. It was pretty late for any plans for scholarship seeking or admission essay writing. It was a mess. And individual student lives were being impacted. Futures. Potentials. Abhorrent. But neither Ms. Betty Jane nor I spent much time opening files and shaking our heads in dismay. Neither of us was into the victim act or any drama queen behavior. We literally rolled up our sleeves, opened a large bag of peanut m&ms and began to restore an order where there had been none for quite some time.

Ms. Betty Jane gets full credit for the filing reorganization in my book. Oh sure, I made some efforts, but then there was the line of students waiting constantly to see me about everything from their suicide attempt the night before due to unrequited love, or to complain and ask for help to deal with their parents' insistence they attend college when they wanted to do something completely other, or weep wildly because they failed a critical exam, or beg for scholarship updates, or ask to change a course when it was too late, or ask if I had any extra food, or register a sexual assault, or any number of things many people believe our children ought not to need to deal with at such an age. But that was the reality. It is far worse now.

The absolutely most difficult thing I had to deal with that year was to tell three children that their father had committed suicide. He had actually been an acquaintance of mine, he and his wife and children had me over several times for dinner or afternoon tea, and since all social activity there in North Carolina revolves around "church" I had joined a choir at one and his wife was a fellow alto in the group. He had rigged his exhaust into the truck cab and died without even knowing it. A recovering alcoholic, his wife was relieved that when he was found, though he had a fifth of liquor on the seat next to him, it remained unopened. This was evidently something to hold onto.

This was not my first brush with suicide, not by a long shot, and when his wife came in to tell me and ask me if I would tell the kids, I thought the same thing I always think when we lose a human to depression; he must have been in the deepest of anguish and despair. This is all I really do know from having made some solid suicide attempts myself and waking up anyway; from holding friends before, during, and after a successful suicides. I knew that it is not an easy thing to end one's life. It requires one's complete will, without doubt, as well as the immersion of the entire being into the deepest and darkest of despair. And so this is my "go to" when I need to either let someone know they lost someone they love to suicide, or when I need to process such a loss in my own life as well. I have lost over a dozen former students to suicide in the thirty years I have been working as an educator. The question "why?" doesn't begin to cover my questions. But I have seen the answers in reality and I am well aware that most of us don't want to make the societal or personal changes necessary to create more humane systems that would actually support and regard humans and all life as intrinsically valuable.

One morning shortly after I had added guidance counselor to my repertoire, my choir buddy came into the office, her face ashen and streaked with tears. I could see from Ms Betty Jane's facial expression when she looked into my office to let me know who was here that it was devastating news. I had worked with three of their children fairly closely, especially the two at the high school, and since we were at the high school, those were the two children I told first. Their mum was too paralyzed to speak, had only managed to tell me through broken sobs in a hoarse whisper.

Ms. Betty Jane had already gone to the classrooms and ushered the students to the office so when I opened my door to ask her to fetch them, they were already sitting in the outer office, looking scared and holding hands. I thanked my friend and colleague for her responsiveness and asked them in; when they saw their mum slumped in a chair they went to her quickly both to hold her and to feel safer themselves. Console and be consoled. They had no clue. I had no idea what they were imagining was going on so I asked them to sit down (Ms. Betty Jane had brought in chairs from the outer office as the children came into my office) and I began the way I always begin. This is not a time to weave a statement. There is no reassurance to be found to offer ahead of the announcement. I asked them to have a seat and they pulled the extra chairs over close to their mum's.

"Your father committed suicide early this morning at the new job site," I said as quietly yet clearly as possible, looking from one set of eyes to the other as I spoke in a compassionate yet primarily neutral tone; leave them room for their own emotions. They looked the way we all look when we are given such news: confused and devastated all at once. They looked at me as though I were speaking in an ancient tongue they didn't recognize. "He must have been in terrible pain for quite some time." I said, echoing the fact with the only thing I knew about such things.

They were now completely wrapped around their mum and each other, chairs drawn together into a triangle so close it become a dot, a single tear. I just stood and breathed and waited. Their inevitable questions would begin as soon as they caught their breath. How? Why? When? As though the details matter. But the most critical piece in my mind was to make sure I kept reiterating that it was nothing they had done or not done, that it had nothing to do with their behaviors, that he loved them immeasurably without a doubt. He just couldn't handle taking another breath; the psychological pain, perhaps far more difficult to handle than physical, had become unbearable. That was essential. This was not their cross to carry; their cross would be to forgive him and accept the new reality and adjust; I wanted them to be as free of self-reprisal as possible, free from needing to forgive themselves for something they had or hadn't done and fall into the pit of depression themselves.

I answered their rote questions as they asked them.

"He rigged the truck to bring the exhaust into the cab," I said, "out at the job site for the new house." And another critical piece – "He didn't feel anything in the end."

He hadn't suffered physically or gotten messy in the process which was quite thoughtful. Not everyone creates a plan which attempts to minimize others' pain in discovering the body; not everyone has the time or energy necessary for this. What it told me was that he'd known for a while, been creating a plan for a while, long enough to still have moments of clarity in which he could consider others and plan accordingly. This is rarely the case in my experience; most suicide is a final act of desperation and is not planned at all but rather driven into blindly, completely lost, perceiving the next step as absolutely impossible. And so it is.

I had yet to go to the middle school to speak with youngest of his children in the district, a young man in the fifth grade who had been adopted by them when his own father, my friend's brother in fact, had shot and killed his wife and himself, blowing the then 18-month-old's forearm to smithereens in the process. So this was going to be exponentially more difficult. And it was. And what I knew was that this young man would be dealing with this shit the rest of his life, struggling just to believe he was okay, that he hadn't done anything wrong. And to top it all off, given that both his genetic father and adoptive father (genetic uncle) suffered from depression, it was more than likely a condition he would also need to struggle with throughout life. His work around this would take decades, if it was possible at all. Trauma has a shelf life of three generations when folks actually work on it with a trustworthy therapist; it's endless without being addressed.

Meanwhile, back in the counselor's offices, we got the college applications and scholarship information into order first just so the students who were potentially strong candidates with clear intentions and substantial financial needs could at least still make some of the due dates. But these tasks impacted primarily the seniors, those in their twelfth year, which in the states is the standard graduation year. And we certainly had plenty to do to keep everyone up to date with this process, learning it ourselves as we went.

But the senior year is not the primary year post-secondary most interesting to college and university admissions officers. The junior year is most critical for those hoping to attend college or university, at least in regard to academic performance. The admissions' process has yet to hit full swing for the student, but this is the year in which one must prepare for it. This is the year admissions' officers look most closely at when vetting possible newbies. Why? Mostly to check for a consistency of student's effort, for if an exemplary student is going to show signs of cracking, this is the year within which it most frequently occurs. There is an element of the junior year that few seem prepared for despite that previous generations of college goers have suffered through it in some form and at some point in their own lives.

Folks would call me weeping, wanting to know why their "up until now" perfect child perfect athlete perfect student perfect musician perfect lady or perfect gentleman was not acting accordingly anymore. They were at a loss. All of them. Not just the parental units, but the students who would come sit with me in the office post parent drama call, hunched over or slouching with legs extended to make a rebellious statement, or in tears, lost, unknowing, unable to figure out why they just didn't give a flying fuck anymore. Okay, so it was hard not to laugh in some sort of buddhist joyous celebration with them at the time, but hey, it wasn't what they needed nor were ready for it yet, so it's not where I went. My job was simple in regard to both parents and students: reassure and get them to relax a bit. Oh sure, if they really did wanna get into Duke or something on scholarship then they didn't have much time to twist about on this particular strand of cord. But not many students are confident enough to set their sights that high.

It is not infrequent for folks who reach the age of 16 or 17 in our country who have performed like circus animals for their parents' love and affection and respect and treats all their lives to perhaps open an eye sideways one morning and begin to wonder, begin their now decade-delayed existential crisis. Now, they didn't know why they were working so damned hard, or why they were going in the direction they discovered themselves going in, or the more general, "what the fuck?" rose to the surface of the youngsters' consciousness. The parents frequently claimed to no longer recognize them. Most concerning to the children, they no longer recognized themselves. They just couldn't work themselves up like they could before about exams and projects and grades and "deadlines". Horrified, they awoke to their days and went to sleep at night not caring at all, except perhaps for how it would affect their parents and therefore their precious righteous freedoms. Everyone was miserable at the very least.

This is a precarious dilemma and one in which we can and do lose valuable minds and hearts. In addition, as with all else when working with human beings in a developmental capacity, it must be handled on a personal, individualized basis. No standard operating procedure other than to listen very carefully, listening for openings for what may be possible, listening for fear and shame and other barriers, listen for stress and pressure and confusion and especially loss and grief. Listen for what may be true. And if a youngster has parents highly involved, then they too must be listened to as well for all of the same reasons. Then, strangely enough, listened to intently enough, openly enough, non-judgmentally enough, having as one's only intent to discover what could be done to ease everyone's pain and confusion, the individuals in the family could begin to hear their own ideas and each other's. They would suggest and try to make changes which alleviated what they had discovered was now working against them. Pressuring a child at a certain point may be necessary and effective in getting them to reach for the next rung, but like all else in life, one tool in your carpentry belt just ain't gonna allow much work to progress. Tools must be developed, improved upon, diversified, trued. And one is simply never enough when dealing with human beings.

This was now 2001; colleges and universities had yet to reduce their standards and politicize/monetize their admissions process to today's pathetic degree. Which is not to say it didn't happen. Sons of Yale went to Yale. In North Carolina, the children of those who graduated from UNC did not apply to NC State. Nor the other way around. Oh no. But these schools weren't necessarily pushovers for alumni favors so much as the more prestigious ivy league ones. However, there were still and always will be t's to dot and eyes to cross.

There will also probably still be post-secondary schools in the southern states which are known as "black schools" and in which very few white kids apply. Howard University is currently the most famous of these. As a yankee, I had never heard of such a thing and so I had to quickly learn what was what or else risk offending some white kid's racist parents by suggesting s/z/he apply to a "black school". Or at least to do so knowing what effect it may have ahead of time.

While there, I was told more than once by some of the older black teachers and staff that they had it better when they had their own schools. They believed they got a better education in places where they could just be themselves rather than second rate citizens at best. Perhaps this is at the root of why the churches were almost without exception, considered "black" or "white" and formed accordingly. If I attended a black Baptist service on a Sunday morning, I only got away with it because I had students in the church who made sure everyone knew I was okay before the service began. While there, the students were primarily responsible for teaching me all manner of new cultural subtleties. I learned that there are black and white names, music, dance halls, organizations, geographic areas, eateries, etc. Not everyone in the black community there was evidently into forfeiting their own cultural heritage to join what imagined itself a superior class but which had mere remnants of a culture remaining.

Though I was offered the high school guidance counselor position for the following year, complete with a paid masters in school guidance, I was still searching for home. Still searching for a circle to join – one which I would not need to lead. I was searching for what may be next; I was always looking for the back door as soon as I became too well known, too often commended and complimented, which conflicted with my air tight identity as worthless. In addition, I still had thousands of dollars of debt to pay back from the academy years, and unfortunately North Carolina didn't pay well enough to both live and pay debt. So, I moved on instead of staying. I suppose I wasn't a damn yankee after all.

NORTH OF HARLEM

In the 90s and early years of 2000, folks with too much money decided to buy up vast sections of Harlem and renovate them into upper class yuppie dwellings. This gentrification, which now demanded higher rents and other costs associated with the basics of living, spurred a migration up the Hudson River to the next available rat-infested but affordable city. I got to spend a year there, working with folks ages 14 and 15 years who had never seen a day of their own childhood. The heroin trade moved up river as well, readily available and cheap, as well as all else our society has burdened our working poor and immigrants with that follows them everywhere in such a racist society; African Americans and immigrants from every continent were well represented within and throughout the school where I landed a one year sub position teaching English among other things.

I wore several hats that year as well. I was to teach English classes for a teacher on maternity leave, work with teachers across disciplines as a National Writing Project consultant to help them learn to utilize writing as a learning tool regardless of the specific subject matter, tutored in the after-school program, and thus, make enough money to pay back all of the academy's remaining debts, which were plentiful, l as I had borrowed from everyone I knew to keep the place open as long as I had. Additionally, my habit of moving around as though a target hiding from its certain bullet was an expensive neurosis to support.

I had a great mix of classes that year – honor's English with primarily ESL students and basic English with a couple of crews of kiddos no one else wanted to deal with, ever, if possible. Now these were my people. One of the most dangerous ideas anyone ever has, and unfortunately humans have it a lot – is that we know what we're getting into; we garner strength from the familiar without stopping to consider what, specifically, is familiar – and whether that is a good thing or a bad thing.

The school building was a spiritual black hole. Oh yes, I recognized this scene. I remembered all too well that need to take a deep breath before going through the door and then holding it for as many hours as necessary – breathing shallowly, cautiously the whole day – and then not letting that deep breath go until a safe distance from danger is ensured. Preferably in a locked car blocks away from the building where hell happens daily. Times like these, one's spiritual practices deepen. The only way I made it through the year was by upping the ante on my yoga and meditation practices, as well as my time walking and cycling in nature. The other thing that helped, of course, were the students themselves. After I had been duly tested by their best, and was deemed okay, even "cool" by some, which simply meant I didn't sweat the small stuff. That's all cool ever means.

Once all 800 souls made it through the metal detectors okay, the mornings were full up. I got to oversee a ninth grade homeroom wherein students would argue about which upstate prison they wanted to end up in based on which one had the best food or exercise equipment the way some students might discuss their college or other plans post graduation. But that's usually not until eleventh or twelfth grade, when faced with the impending decisions. These folks were in ninth grade – but none of them expected to get past tenth, or eleventh if they got lucky. They didn't have many options from the wormholes of degradation they and their people had been living in for years, or for some, generations.

My morning classes, both honors English, were comprised primarily of new immigrants studying English as a second language. The folks there in the early part of 2000s came primarily from eastern Europe and the middle east, though many of them were originally from northern Africa. Very few made it there from south or central America, though there were some students representing the state of Puebla in Mexico.

ESL students rock. They're more fully invested in learning that any English-speaking student I've ever had anywhere in the United States. And this was no different. There were some students there who represented the general demographic of what I was finding public school honors classes were comprised of – primarily the more affluent white kids, even when they were immigrants. As long as their daddies were white and had money, it seemed they had a more immediate value for the schools to invest in. If the students had intentions of "getting somewhere," which meant out of town forever, preferably via a decent university with a fat scholarship, the school had more of an Immediate investment. This is just one of the many ways the capitalistic spirit infiltrates our schools and teaches our children that production and payment matter most.

Of course, there were the smattering of the brilliant weirdo artist types, (which, in 2003, meant primarily "goths"), who may be the least well served, most frequently "lost" students in the system, often struggling with deeper existential issues than simply identity, including sexuality and gender. They are also some of the hungriest learners, most brilliantly imaginative minds, and most often lost early to suicide or drugs. Or both.

And then, in the afternoon, I got to work with a couple of groups of people for whom the entire thing was a joke but the Welfare and Medicaid checks get cut off if the student is absent too often, or their parole or probation could be jeopardized. For some, recently released from rehab or jail, school was non-negotiable. So there we were. Post cafeteria lunch which is all sugar and carbs, in a hot classroom on the third floor of a rat-infested building with a couple of dozen kiddos who were 14 or 15 years of age going on 80 or 48, but not ever 16.

Once I passed all their tests and we figured each other out, we had a great time. But with kiddos who live in a war zone, this can take a while. This demands that they be worn down, so to speak, and this demands one be as real as possible with students. It demands humanity, humility and courage all at once. It cannot be about becoming their buddy or pal; this never, ever works out; this ego driven dynamic blurs absolutely essential boundaries that the student must be able to rely upon. That "lemme be your friend" thing goes straight to hell quickly every time. I myself am a firm believer in tough love as a vital remedy. Sadly, not many folks have friends trusted enough to tell each other the difficult and uncomfortable truths. Not many folks are invested in the truth to the degree necessary to break through the effort required. And it can't just be tough, it must also be unconditional. Any parent or relative who has raised a child from a sprout knows unconditional love can be tested to the point of breakage. Though holding fast to it can be difficult as hell, it is as vital as it is difficult.

By now I had done quite a bit of reading regarding children, trauma, and possibilities; what I knew even more thoroughly now was it only requires one human being who truly cares to make a difference in a child's life. One person. Anyone. Just so they believe in the child and do not falter in their love, which is not a mushy love, but the kind that demands we each and all stand up and become who we truly are. This is all I hoped to offer; it was all I really had for these kiddos. Which was fine, as it was all they really needed.

At this particular school in this particular neighborhood, there was a daily lockdown for one reason or another; usually accompanied by police and dawgs and searching and arresting. Never quietly. It was not unusual to stand outside in the rain or cold for hours before the school was sufficiently swept for whatever they'd gotten an alert about. Once it was permissible to enter, there were the many metal detectors to go back through, and after everyone was inside all manner of weaponry – fancy and homemade – could be found in the bushes outside the front door. As well as some other interesting merchandise. One of the students' favorite games was to pull the fire alarm and then when we were all outside standing in our assigned areas in the parking lot, they'd have a great time running about touching or banging on the expensive cars to elicit the alarm to sound. Given the class time amounted to 37 minutes, students frequently went outside with a class and then simply gathered together with their friends and hang out somewhere in the grounds or wander off for a while to get stoned. What a zoo.

In the basement was a room I named the seventh circle where I got to spend a couple of hours a week, as did every teacher without tenure. It was an assigned duty. Which consisted of spending 37 minutes in a small room without windows or any natural light at the end of a long hall in the basement with myriad students sent by teachers for, according to most of the slips I received, "not cooperating in class". They showed up and had to sit with whatever teacher was cursed that day, for the duration of the class period. This was particularly interesting when a teacher would send a couple of students down who had been fighting in class; not arguing, fighting, throwing punches as well as whatever was handy and hitting hard, often from battling gangs. Given that most teachers really have no training or personal experience with children who have nothing left to lose, many students who had no control at all were relegated to this room before they got into the classroom just as I had been relegated to my little desk in the principal's office.

So amidst this already spiritual black hole, here was a dank dark old storage room that I recognized from Ursula LeGuin's short story, "The Ones Who Walk Away from Omelas". The only difference was it was a big closet with multiple children inhabiting it at any one time, rather than the broom closet with one. I recognized the place though I had never been in the building before. I also recognized the children; it was like looking in a mirror twenty or even thirty years ago. Here were the sacrificial lambs; here were the children who had been tossed, given up on, relegated to the basement so that all of the others could get on with "it", whatever "it" may be. I swear to gawd it was a war zone. Everyone was on hyper alert, hyper drive. Helpless. Hopeless.

Some folks would somehow find a place and a way to be there in the school, which is much more possible if you are smart, talented in arts or athletics, or, as it was now 2003, experiencing a sexual or gender situation which was zany enough to be cool. The gal who would have been treated like shit, ostracized, and deemed a "lesbo" in 1970 had become a different matter; now, LGBTQ kiddos had a friggin' club to belong to. They had rights and knew them and flouted themselves and their rights everywhere. And somewhere along the line, by being just as strange and shocking as they wished, they'd earned the relegation of "cool". We had indeed come a long way baby. Or at least our children had.

In all fairness to my fellow teacher people, let me say it is a real tragedy that we demand our teachers be a teacher as well as a therapist and parent and social worker and gawd knows what else may be needed… nurse, counselor, confidante, security guard… there is very little learning going on because there is minimal teaching time. In these situations, which blanket our nation's inner city schools in particular, there is time needed to make sure everyone is okay – fed and watered and pottied if you will, as it is fruitless and well, stupid, to start any class if you're about to have 37 interruptions in that many minutes. And that is all the minutes we had to work with remember. 37. You must immediately cut 3 to 10 minutes off at the beginning for getting settled in, depending on myriad particulars. Taking time to get settled in and checked in is always a sound investment because even once they are settled in, they are very much alive and charged up and looking for all kinds of things to invest their attentions in other than an education. Try conveying to any child anywhere essential information in 37 minutes or less in a small usually dark and damp Copperfieldian room whilst at least a couple dozen more of their classmates scream, throw things, puke, suck face, check make-up, throw cigarettes or lipstick across the room, arrange and rearrange penises and balls and boobs, copy homework, ad infinitum, ad nauseum. If you don't begin with some fragment of peace and order, everyone in the room is certainly screwed for the next 37 minutes. It ain't pretty.

I had a deep and abiding aversion to sending anyone to the basement Hades and so I never did. I did tell students to leave if they weren't capable of being civil, but I let them take their chances with the authorities and security out in the hall. They needed to leave because they were acting in a way that was hurtful to themselves or others. That was my line – kindness. I don't care where you come from or what's going on, there is never a good reason to be mean and nasty. All family feuds and gang shit ended at the doorway. Period. I was strict about this but of course many had to test me to find that out. Fortunately, I have a thing about keeping my word.

It was the same aversion I had to everything about the inhumane system known as public education in this country. The same aversion I had to an entire society that devalued everything truly essential about being human, that put a price tag on everything, that assiduously forced humans of any depth into a hell it was nigh impossible to crawl out of, then blamed those humans for their frailty or genuineness or even the traumatization the society itself had caused. The clear fact is that in our society, perhaps in all of human societies, the victim must carry and bare the shame. Every time. This devastates our most sensitive, empathic, insightful, and creative folks; it is not uncommon for them to eventually succumb to suicide.

I always learn more than I teach. Always. At least, when I am open to listening, and not just trying to make a point, or stick to a plan. Actually, I teach because it is one of the contexts I have discovered in life where it's pretty critical to discover the point, explore the possibilities, and plan but only enough to create a framework with enough flexibility for something real to occur. My students have always taught me far more than I have taught them. Always.

One of my lifelong adages has been that the only thing I really know is that I don't know, and I must admit that I continue to learn this; I am always surprised by what's true and real. Another adage is that I am not a teacher because I have the answers, but because I have more questions than the students do, and I don't care how foolish I look sharing them out loud.

What I am usually modeling is simply being human, human in that messing up and caring and sometimes not that is often more tragic than joyous if one can't grow from the tragedies. There was never anything a student brought to me as a rationale for not being themselves, for not learning, for suffering rather than strengthening, for killing themselves, that I could not look them in the eye and say from a place of experience within myself, "nope." If I was still here on the planet, still striving, so could they. I suppose in this I afforded some of them inspiration and drive. And I did not waste energy pretending to be anything else – I came from these same streets and here I was. So no excuses. No victim acts. No matter what. Another valuable aspect I modeled was when I would catch myself pretending and calling myself on it with everyone watching. Because we're not here to do anything else, but be as real as we can be.

Teachers are frequently called out into the hallway for countless reasons during any given class time. When one opens the door to the classroom, well, let's just say most students I taught in public schools weren't yet capable of making sound choices for themselves and so, zoo time. I would simply stand in the doorway as I had learned as a child that yelling upon yelling does not create clarity or quiet but more chaos and insanity. I would stand there in the doorway watching them until someone noticed me standing there. Then, as with all herd behavior, one by one all of their eyes would look and stare and wonder. I would wait for absolute silence, and sometimes that could take a while, but nothing else was going to resolve the scene so what the hell.

One day as I was standing there a student, once it was quiet, asked loudly, "Hey! What's up miss?"

I answered his question with another one for all of the students as I moved into the room. "So what you're all telling me is that you need some old white lady to tell you what to do or you turn into cartoon characters in a shitty graphic novel that goes nowhere?" I paused and let them furrow their brows. I could see the struggle on some faces. Had I just put them down, or myself? Hmmm. Then I continued. "Hey, if that's what you wanna practice and get good at, go for it, by all means. After all, we get excellent at whatever we practice, so if you wanna use your time on your own to pull yourself and your buds down, I'm sure you'll get it down to a fine art and then you can wake up at age forty to go to a job or worse where you take orders from some old white lady or guy and then go out for a beer with your peeps to complain about your shitty life. Or maybe you could practice investing in yourself and in so doing give all the stupid bossy old white people the finger." Of course this got some laughter, but they heard me. I could see it moving through them individually and communally. Then one student, the one in every classroom who can always be counted on to lighten the tension, did just that.

"Ahhh, yeah but you ain't white ms," he said.

I will admit my heart swelled with joy, yet I denied his observation initially.

I grabbed a bunch of skin on my forearm and said, "This is white skin bro; I be a white woman."

He laughed. "Naw, you know what I mean ms.," he looked about conspiratorially for assent votes and got a bunch of head nods. "You ain't like no old white lady we ever met."

My heart swelled again and I went with it.

"Sir," I responded, as I always addressed the students with the same respect the system demanded they exhibit toward teacher people, "I am not exactly sure why at this moment but that is one of the nicest things anyone has ever said to me. Thank you." I allowed myself a smile of gratitude to them all, then moved on. "Now let's get back to work, eh?"

And we did. For real.

Near the end of the school year I decided to give students a test on literary terms. It was a model public school test; one of a handful I have ever made and given in my life. Multiple guess, fill in the blanks, and an essay for those who wanted extra credit. Given their classwork had been more portfolio based, I wanted to see how they would do with a formal exam which they would ultimately need to take should anyone wish to go somewhere other than prison or rehab. And even there, tests await.

Foreshadowing occurred in the first period honors' class. Wasn't even a quarter to eight in the morning and already they were letting me know. Jonathan, who had to work so hard to pretend he was dumb that he literally sweat, took one look at the test, arched both eyebrows and said, "This ain't like you miss."

Of course, and sadly, I chose to ignore the first sound of truth made since it was gonna mess up a decision to which I had already committed myself. With the state-based final exam looming on the horizon, it was time to see if their knowledge would translate readily to multiple guesswork. If not, we'd need to do some work specifically on that.

So, instead of listening to the voice of reason via Jonathan, I quipped back. "I'm trying to work out of my box right now Jonathan… get a pencil from the drawer and go take the test."

He shrugged, smiled, and complied. That first period group had some degree of public school enculturation. A test is serious business. Far more serious than learning, or caring. Anyway. The rest of the day wasn't such a big deal. Students took "the test" and I took the opportunity to read and respond to a stack of their journals a zillion miles deep.

Then came ninth period. Ninth period, with Mr. Q, the G-man, Natasha, Nhatosha and TaiMai, Peter and Penny, and the two Nadenes. One look at the test and it was total bedlam. And what I immediately knew was, they weren't doing it. Oh, I talked them through part one, the multiple choice part, and with some cheerleading they managed that part. But as they arrived at part two, it became clear even to me that this wasn't going any further.

They wanted a "word bank". They said it was "unfair". They claimed it made no sense. Initially, I countered their objections with my own. The word bank is the terms in part one. Not good enough, too much work to find. I said my usual thing about life not being fair – one of my more ridiculous defense mechanisms. Preaching to the choir too; these young people and I come from Unfair Street. We knew it wasn't fair out there. We were hoping it could be fair in here somewhere, dammit.

I watched as they began to shut down. Oh, Nadene G. and Andrew could pull it off; they had a combination of intelligence and confidence rare within these walls and that allowed them to keep at something no matter what. But Jamar shut down completely. I watched as his anger at "not getting it" suffused into his whole being. His pen dropped loudly onto his desk. He glared out into the rain-pained window. His hands become fists. Tai Mai put on her poker face and started snapping her gum loudly, sharply, like a slap every time. Peter and Penny kept at it, never looking up, pretending not to listen to the others' grumbling. They were faking it, guessing and pretending they knew, refusing to let anyone wonder if they were okay. It had been working for them for years. Shanika liberated her cell phone from the bottom of her purse by spilling its contents onto the floor and asked if she could call her Godmother. I am no longer losing them. I have lost.

Mr Q puts on his smooth and says, "Tell ya what miss, why don'tcha just count part one?" he glanced about conspiratorially while mysteriously maintaining eye contact with me. "No one else has ta know," he whispered, smiling.

At that exquisite and torturous place where expectation meets reality and crumbles, I stood, quivering. Knowing only that I was, once again, lost, and that if I was to be found, if any good could be salvaged from this, everything must be up for grabs. Everything. Including yet another of my ideas about what was needed from me by others.

I took a deep breath and said again, rather mechanically now, and certainly with more question than conviction, "All the other classes did it."

Natasha is all over that one. "You can't go comparing us to other classes," she reminds me. "That ain't right miss."

"But if it was too hard, or unfair, everyone would've had trouble with it," I countered. Natasha and I knew this was no longer an argument, but a conversation. And the rest of the students, now listening intently to every sound and watching every gesture, were hanging onto it like a life-saving rope.

"Still," Natasha shakes her head sadly, almost disparagingly, "It ain't right miss – everyone's different."

Too true a statement for denial. So I did what I do when I'm lost in a group of people. "What do y'all think we should do?" I ask.

Mr. Q was all over it. "Let's do part two together!!!" he shouted joyously, as though discovering a treasure trove of weed in a Broadway Avenue pothole.

"Did'ja'll study?" I sighed, sensing my shoulders droop.

"Swear to gawd, ms – I actually did study – I know this stuff," Mr Q asserted rather vivaciously.

"He does," TaiMai offered some credibility, checking for it in the quality of her most recent fingernail polish art, and added, "he was actually goin' over 'em at lunch and he got 'em almost all right."

"Okay," I sighed.

I sat on the desk, and we read through part two together. And it turned out they did know the answers. And when I listened to some of the sentences through their ears, I heard how some of the fill in the blanks were too amorphous, even unfair. And they heard out loud through my ears that they knew more than they thought they knew. And I learned, once again, what I should already maybe have known, or was at least reminded of what really matters. And they saw for a moment that maybe something different could happen here, that something in life could be fair, and real, and human.

Later that night as I sat correcting my perfect little exam, I discovered that I had to disclude the part two scores for every class. Though most of the students went ahead and either guessed or blew off part two, absolutely no one did well on it, and it brought their scores down to a miserable and often failing grade. Not because they didn't know the material, but because I had not created a test that wasn't fair, or clear, or even possible. So, despite Mr. Q's suggestion that no one need know that I wasn't going to count part two, everyone did know, as I handed back the exams the next day, and explained the scores to every class, letting them know that I cancelled out part two because it was not a fair exam. And letting them know how the folks in ninth period had stood up for themselves and persevered and taught me a thing or two in the process.

I have a dear friend who has taught three- and four-year-olds for over 40 years now. When we were younger and closer geographically, every September and sometimes in January as well, she would visit me after school and tell me which of her new students was to be "her teacher" for the term. She always described the child and told stories from the day to illustrate exactly how this little person (or small animal as she often referred to them) was going to test her limits and demand she grow and improve as a teacher and human being.

The students in this ninth period class came to trust me enough to come to me with their more urgent concerns; everyone knew I came in early, was available during lunch, and stayed late. Everyone knew I could keep my mouth shut when it mattered most. As I said, I had been tested and passed.

It was during one such lunch period that Mr Q and Natasha dashed into the little classroom, yelling excitedly about home economics class and cooking and an dropping an egg and, "Oh my gawd ms there was fuckin' blood in it!" Natasha got to the point briskly by pushing through Mr Q's prelude.

I had to smile. City kids. I used to be one of them, though not as removed from the planet and its critters as these kiddos now were. Neither of these students missed much so they demanded to know why I was smiling.

"It was probably fertile," I shrugged slightly and turned back to the journal to which I'd been responding. Then I smiled again, waiting.

"What the fuck are you talking about?" yelled Mr Q, while Natasha, all of 14 years old and beginning to show at the fifth month of her pregnancy, just stood there completely perplexed.

He had to repeat himself as I wasn't quick enough for him. "What the fuck, ms?" He may have been holding his breath.

I put my green pen down and stood up to meet their eyes at a more level stance. Then I said it again. "I said, it was probably fertile," I repeated more directly this time. "Lemme ask you guys something, okay? Where do eggs come from?"

Mr Q rolled his eyes and slapped his thighs in disbelief at my own ignorance. "Everyone friggin knows that," he said, "they come from the friggin' grocery store."

"Any store, really," added Natasha, specifiying, "I get 'em for my gramma at Dollar General. They have everything."

Now I worked to not smile. "Okay," I said simply, but raising my hands to the sky as though a request for some immediate grace. I sat on a desk and they stood in front of me, poised, ready to receive the vital information to solve the puzzle. "Listen," I said, teacherly, "eggs come from chickens, chickens come from eggs."

They stared at my face, looking lost, quizzical, needing more specifics.

I looked at Natasha and said, "This may be exactly why you're prego, dearheart," then to them both, again, more slowly so the shock would be lessened if possible. "Eggs are essentially chicken menstruation and you must have gotten one somehow that was fertilized by a rooster. Not so easy to do these days given the way they keep them."

Before I had finished my explanation, Mr Q was on the floor writhing, all six feet and four inches of his scrawny self. His hands about his throat, he was screaming that he'd never eat another egg in his life. I reminded him amidst his drama that they were in pretty much everything he ate – cookies, bread, etcetera. He continued to writhe, though with less passion as time passed and he wore himself out. Meanwhile, Natasha just stood there, her little baby belly in her hands, staring out the window. I leaned toward her to get eye contact but she looked down to the floor where Mr Q was doing his best to maintain his disgust now about the fact that he could no longer eat anything with eggs in it, and she kicked him in the ribs lightly. "Let's go," she said, "I wanna grab a smoke before lunch is over."

"I'm here if you need more information sweetie," I whispered to Natasha on their way out the door.

"You didn't have to say it that way," she retorted, justly. "You didn't have to be so mean and crude."

Checked again by the integrity of youth, I responded earnestly, "You're right Natasha; I promise not to be so crude if you need more information. About anything."

"Whatever," she shrugged, walking away. "Whatever."

This ninth period class served as my teacher of all teachers that year. It demanded everything, which meant it afforded everything. The only trick, as usual, was to refuse to take anything personally and be more concerned with the students for real, as humans becoming; to remain unflaggingly true to that. If the children and their well-being, their education, is the intention, then why on earth would a teacher imagine that they have any right to insert themselves and their own emotional neediness into the equation? In fact, their responsibility is actually to model emotional impartiality when it is appropriate to do so in the service of others. Students need to see this as a responsible way to behave. Don't drag your drama and dirt everywhere; it simply doesn't make it possible for anything more real to occur if everyone is literally paying their attentions to the drama.

But more positive emotional experiences can also be modeled, such as joy and pleasure and self awareness. There are times in a classroom when something can occur that is so genuinely excellent there is no way a human teacher can keep from practicing playfulness or exhibiting happiness; nor should they, lest our children continue to grow up thinking adulthood is a boring place where we've forfeited all our fun for some idea of a future.

When I first arrived in this school to teach English and Honors English, I could find no book room, no books. I went to the principal and asked about the procedure to acquire books at his school. He laughed at me. "These children can't read," he laughed, dismissing my clear ignorance with a wave of his mighty hand. "Your students are probably reading at a third grade level at best. What do you think you're going to get them to read?"

I just stood there, as if waiting to see if this was just a flashback from some old movie or book I had read about this being said. I was not the first to hear it, nor was the principal the first to say it. For all I knew, he himself had been told the same information and actually believed it.

"Well," I responded finally when the silence became a bit awkward, "It is difficult to read without a book." And I just turned and walked out. This guy was just another useless administrator who may or may not have ever done time as a classroom teacher himself. I had better things to do, things that might actually help the kiddos improve their reading. First, I had to find material for them to read, then I had to get them to actually read it when such things hadn't been expected before and were certainly not anticipated by my students now, not after years of being told they couldn't read. Now I was demanding they could? Should? Had to? Or as one young man in the honors English class so aptly responded on the day I handed out the books I had created by making 100 copies of it on the school copy machine along with the 100 blank composition book journals I had purchased myself.

"What the fuck ms?" he wanted to know.

"It's a solid read; you'll like it; I promise."

The honors classes adjusted well with some students really going for it with this reading response journal stuff; I had trouble responding to so many so completely and began to minimize my own responses more just to get enough time to be able to respond sincerely with questions and concerns, to make some tiny bit of communication possible was all that they really needed and I had to learn, yet again, to slow down, back down, demand less of myself so there was enough of me to go around and last through the year.

The students in my afternoon classes were another matter. I had a few of the book copies left over from the morning classes but I didn't think most of the folks in these classes would be into the book I had chosen for the earlier classes. These kiddos came from a different place then the morning students. They also needed more diverse variety to choose from. While honor students generally like to be told exactly what to do and how to do it and when it's due, most students do not like this at all. For many of the afternoon students, being told what to do by a strange adult authority figure just wasn't gonna work at all. After all, who the hell was I anyway? They got enough of this shit from their POs and grammas and rehab therapists and social workers. I could already hear their response to the entire idea of reading and responding as an integral part of our class time in my own head and in my own young voice, "Fuck off" it muttered bitterly. It was concise.

I didn't know what to expect so I did what I do and got behind it with all the zest and enthusiasm I could muster. And I somehow made it possible, "legal" in their terminology, to read whatever they wanted as long as it wasn't x-rated and had more words than pictures. Magazines were legal, which meant they could just read about whatever interested them. Was I tested here as well? Of course I was. My students were not stupid by any stretch, just poor as dust; however they had been taught and learned through and through that they were stupid by some very stupid people.

This is problematic, and at its core is the core problem with schools throughout the country. Without a real education themselves regarding awareness, mindfulness, selflessness, community mindedness, the mysteries of nature and our responsibility therein, how on earth can teachers be expected to convey it to the next generation? How does a person supersede their own education and training to become more true to themselves? Supersede an entire system's value system when they were educated by that very system? What happens to a civilization that loses the vital knowledge and practices that allow us to remember who we are and what we are doing here? That forfeits presence for popularity? Can such a strand ever be caught again? Can it ever be rewoven into life's daily fabric? Teachers must accept the responsibility to educate themselves beyond the scope afforded by their previous formal education; teachers who do so are rarely at a complete loss in the classroom and less likely to "burn out". They also frequently yield the joyous results of students changing and growing by affording a safe yet more flexible, creative framework in which to work for children who have rarely had such an experience. They also do so often at great expense to themselves and their own life.

The ninth period class had the great benefit of a couple of students who were gifted writers and had used books and libraries as safe places in which to hide as traumatized children will often do. This was beneficial not merely because they were into such things – had they been other than who they were, they could very well have been teased and denounced for such things. But to my and the entire class's great fortune, they were considered "cool" by the rest of the students and thus, with some accessory street red in my corner, critical mass was present and my job became much much easier. But not easy mind you. Some folks are too far gone to care who other people think are cool. They're busy with other shit; sometimes literally, as one of my students did who stayed and took care of her gramma in hospital at night who was there dying of AIDs. Or the young man who had killed his father for beating and raping his mother one time too many and was up on felony charges. Some folks had moved on from cool in early childhood or even infancy.

For these kiddos, it was vital I both respect them as adults and care for them as children.

Certainly not my first rodeo though, so we figured it out, one by one, slowly but surely working together to find something interesting for each student to read, in class, three days a week for as long as I could keep them at it. Initially, it was perhaps a few minutes of reading for every several minutes of complaining and diversionary tactics. But eventually, slowly, it became possible for them to read their individual books and stories and magazines for up to fifteen minutes in a stretch, in which I was able to also respond to some of their response journals in which they could say anything they wanted about what they were reading.

One rainy afternoon the students for whatever reason came in, read what I had written on the board, which was simply a quote I thought they may enjoy and then the word READ in all caps and many colors of chalk. They either pulled their reading material and journals from their bags or back pockets or went to where they had it stashed in the room and sat down and started reading. And reading. And reading. Half an hour went by and I didn't say a word, though I did keep looking up sometimes, startled by the silence, and smiled warily as I went back to my own work. Evidently, Natasha also noticed.

"Holy fuck miss," she yelled across the room. "Check it out; Hangman is reading!"

I looked up quickly to quiet her down before peace could became bedlam. I gave her a severe look, clearly saying stop with my expression and mouthing the words as though she were unable to hear. But it was already too late to stop her.

"Seriously miss," she allowed, "check it out – everyone is reading, EVERYONE," she attempted to convey her surprise by getting louder and more exuberant. "Check this shit out!" she finalized her point by pointing to a young man who usually slept or drew through class. "Ya got Mr Q reading now!"

"Yes, Natasha, everyone WAS reading," I agree with some level of sadness that it had to end.

By now Natasha was standing up, her hands on her growing hips, staring around the circle of desks at her class-mates, many now captured by her enthusiasm. "We could be one of them tv shows," she said with deep reverence to her classmates. Then she looked up at me, "You're like that fuckin' Mr Kotter guy on tv! We could make a movie! We could be in a show!"

I had to smile. All the students were staring from Natasha to me, not clear about what was going on as they had just been yanked from their reading bubbles.

"A movie?" I asked.

"Yeah," she confirmed, "A fuckin' movie! With us as the stars!"

"Hmmm," I pretended to think out loud for a moment though I always had this response at hand for any student with an enthusiastic idea, "I guess you better write us a script then Ms Natasha."

She beamed. "Maybe I just will," she grabbed at the idea with a swagger. "Maybe I'll just show you all a thing or two."

And she sure did.

THE BORDERLANDS

I knew the gig in the city was simply a one-year permanent sub position from the get go which meant that in April and May I needed to begin to seriously consider what was next. In the time since I had left the academy, I'd played a few more roles. I had done a half year stint in the middle range of the Rockies in an upscale district high school on the wrong side of the creek working with teacher people to develop more creative, integrated curriculum, particularly in the expressive arts. I spent the remainder of the year helping out at an upstate home school group a couple of the academy's teacher people had formed in which I never did find my place. Then there was the year in the city school. I had a penchant for looking around to see what may be needed by folks that I could step-in and provide, and then off I would go, dragging and pushing myself about in an attempt to always serve others without any sense of my own needs, for I had been gifted by my all-too-Irish catholic mum with a core belief that unless we are at the service of others' we have no right to draw a breath. But then there was an even more misguided notion that propelled me to always know where the back door was and to bolt before I would most certainly be found out and tossed. This regardless of my "success" now within the confines of the system. I sometimes moved on simply because I became too well known and valued within the community; that simply meant the fall could go further. I was fueled by the "imposter syndrome".

In my searching, I went to a meditation retreat in Kentucky one weekend and met some women who worked at a school on the border of the United States and Mexico for young women primarily from Mexico; for the most part, those from the US side of the border had not been here very long either. I was still exuberant about the academy experience and my enthusiasm about young folks and education was apparent as we shared stories over meals and walks. I returned to New York and a week later was called for an interview as a teacher and spiritual mentor/guide in their school. I have a thing about trusting the universe despite all of the ugliness I have gotten to walk through; primarily because every time I get tossed by a storm, I learn and grow and get to have experiences and step into situations I could never have dreamt up on my own. I was hired over the phone after what was more of a protocol phone call than an interview. Evidently my creative take on curriculum and my passion for education had been obvious enough in Kentucky to reach the southern border. And so it goes. And so, I went. Yet again, I packed my stuff into whatever shabby vehicle I was depending on at the time and along with whatever critters were depending on me, and I left. From upstate New York yet again, for a bit more sun and culture shock than North Carolina had provided. I was heading to the desert now. The borderlands. Its own land, belonging to no country, no nation. Its only creed: survival.

I had an amazing classroom the first year – it was huge and old and airy with old oak cabinets everywhere in one of the oldest buildings in the city, having been carved from the desert for the young women more than a century ago. The room had a back door into a "secret book room" which was neither secret nor did it contain books. We turned it into a meditation and yoga space that spring after the students had asked me to lead a regular yoga class and a morning meditation circle. I always get where I need to be as early as possible, to give myself a chance to get oriented before the onslaught of needs that walks in the door with every growing human I've ever met. The young women would amble in early as well and keep coming. They would come in, sit in the "weeping chair", a cozy chair at the side of my desk facing me, or lie in clumps about the carpeted floor sharing stories, or gather at one of the tables together and hunch over doing or copying homework. If I wasn't needed, I would work on journals. Yes, I was still committed to such a process. Recitation and writing. Meditation, Lost arts to some; essential to me.

That first year in the desert was truly a year in the desert for me; not in the sense of being starved, but in my own spiritual journeying. There is nowhere to hide in the desert; nothing between a person and the divine spark within everything, including one's self. I had an interesting mix of students as the school's demographics was across the spectrum from fully committed academically to fully committed spiritually to needing to be committed. Though to be fair, the faculty people, those who I suppose were to have their faculties about them, were more committed to an old picture of traditional education and were invested in some strange political faculty drama I never did figure out. Not many had faculties anywhere to be found, for they made no room in their life for any regular practices that might actually cultivate what we were preaching mattered – awareness, kindness, creativity, compassion. You get the picture. Do as I say, not as I do never rang true to me, and it didn't ring true to the young women who gathered in the secret room to meditate each morning and who came on Tuesday afternoons after school for a yoga session as well.

In between, I taught a bunch of different English classes – what are crudely referred to as the "crap classes" by the folks who would rather not teach them. The classes were comprised of all the freshwomen, both the regular and honors version; and all the seniors who had never been interested in anything academic and had had at least one foot out the door and on their car gas pedal's since their quinceaneras years ago.

The freshies were delightful, some wide eyed, some barrio tough, all of them still young enough to want to learn, old enough that they wanted to question everything. The seniors varied widely, from students with learning hindrances or accelerated interests in academics, those who would do anything to learn just to please someone else, those whose walls had already been well and firmly built around their hearts and souls, one of each possible learning style and attitude.

For me, teaching English Literature and Writing is really a matter of teaching the human stories that may reveal something to us of what we may be doing here, who we may be as humans attempting to become, how our societies have evolved and devolved; so, philosophy if you will. These young women had incredible sensibilities and sensitivities to spirituality and injustice, not surprising given how many of them had come from deeply religious and spiritual families with roots in rituals hundreds of years old. There is nothing like celebrating Dia de Muerde on the border, which in reality takes a month at least, and I have never before encountered an entire society so steeped in culture that all 12 days of Christmas counted enough that no one ever scheduled the return for spring term until after January 7th.

Also not surprising that they were interested in justice issues, for most crossed an international border bridge every morning and risked tardiness due to some incident "at the bridge" simply for being a brown person who speaks Spanish and wants to come into the "best nation in the world". Many of them were duly terrified for their lives due to the escalation of rape and murder of young women in their native neighboring city during those years. They weren't able to leave home without another person, preferably a brother or male cousin, though another woman would do in a pinch; the young women held hands tightly wherever they went. Some had fathers or uncles or brothers who had been enticed by the Spanish spoken adverts running throughout the states of Mexico promising excellent job opportunities by US growers and meatpackers and dressmakers and many had returned with at least one severe injury, one less limb or worse; broke, depressed, useless in a land where work demanded two strong arms and legs, needing now to be supported himself, perhaps even taken care of until death. Many were frequently accosted on their way to the bridge by dealers aka gang members who had the policia in their pockets, who threatened them and their families if they would not carry whatever goods they had in the backpack across the border and deliver it on the other side. The fact was that there were times it was not wise or even feasible to refuse them, and they would end up having to mule contraband across in their book bags. Trauma was a daily event for many. Some lived with relatives who had gotten into the US for work, and they knew first hand about borderland issues no one outside of it seems to comprehend well, if at all.

Additionally, despite all the trauma, or maybe due to it in some way, students from Mexico and Central America still had a culture wherein family - children and elders in particularly - were still valued and revered. And they were not taught that the material world and spiritual world are separate worlds, but as overlapping worlds which often if not always touched into each other's spheres. Boundaries if you will, mattered not. There are hundreds of stories and books by Mexican, Central American, ad South American writers and illustrators who speak of and to this weaving, and so we delved into material that might be more interesting for our students, material that spoke more of and to their own experiences and beliefs and existential questions, and their writing assignments demanded much introspection in order to discover and explain how the characters and situations in the literature related to them and their own lives personally.

I suppose my penchant for discussing the human mind, heart, and soul led the higher ups to ask me to teach the following year, but instead of English, it would be an assortment of classes, two AP Psych, in which I was able to share some of what I was learning at the local university as

I had been accepted into a graduate program in Educational Psychology and was enrolled in several night classes. I also got to teach subjects such as comparative religions and justice issues, which hadn't been taught previously so absolutely no curriculum guidelines to check off and it was open season. The school had a fairly decent book budget which I made good use of that year. There were plenty of books stocking one large shelf which included the holy texts from all the major world religions and plenty of material regarding the more peripheral as well as they indigenous belief systems. There was a case of books to read at will regarding every possible subject about the issues I thought may be valuable for young women of their ages and inclinations. Another shelf held classroom copies of the primary books we would be using as a larger group. Though they had moved me to another classroom downstairs, it was still beautifully ancient with plenty of built-in shelves. I had a blast filing them with books, empty journals, and art supplies.

Unfortunately, despite all the incredible young women hungry to learn and grow at the school, I was having more and more trouble holding my life-long depression and anxiety at bay and began to fray at the corners emotionally. I sought out a therapist and when I walked in and had a seat in her office waiting room for the first appointment and looked about at the framed degrees and certificates on the walls, I realized I was in the office of a therapist who specialized in trauma. My stomach dropped as my heart moved into my throat. Yep, that pesky universe was at it again.

Still, despite my illness and my teaching and my school work and my attempt to keep up with my own birth daughter (and several others I had taken care of for months or years when a safe home wasn't something they had available) who had hit their twenties, the decade that young folks make their biggest, most expensive, and lasting mistakes. I had been exhausted a decade ago, believed then all my reserves had been spent. Now, I was way beyond exhausted.

Sadly, I didn't know how to slow down, let alone stop. And my default setting to overwork to prove I was okay went into overdrive. But somewhere inside I knew this was it. I had spent a lifetime helping others do their critical work; it was time to do my own. But I had yet to realize just how empty I was; how little I had to offer anymore; how impossible it would be for me to continue helping anyone until I finally felt I too had a right, even a responsibility, to address my own barriers to learning. In my case it was learning and accepting that I was in pain and had been for decades, that I was a survivor of every kind of abuse in the books, that I did not need to serve others to breathe, and ultimately, that even I was intrinsically valuable.

Though I had planned to return to the school and had signed a contract to teach the same smorgasbord of classes for the following autumn term, when the young women returned from their senior trip, several came to me privately and told me of some events which occurred during the trip which qualified as sexual abuse and needed to be addressed immediately with the adults responsible. However, when I reported it to the schools' president, I was instead made a sacrificial lamb. And when I saw they cared more about their reputations that the students, I made a report myself to Child Protective Services and wrote my letter of resignation. It was very sad.

Leaving yet again, essentially, despite that I'd been the one to write the letter, I had already been dismissed; for caring, for drawing a line of intolerance, for demanding the school accept responsibility and act accordingly. And now what? In the borderlands with no job, bills arriving, no real friends yet, grad school unfinished. This time the back door turned out to be right down the road, in a public school poised literally on the border highway between the US and Mexico in the barrio.

The school I transferred over to was what was at the precipice of being labeled a "priority school" by the state and federal government based on student test scores. A few years before I had arrived, the school principal had sued the all holy border patrol for trespassing and actually won. About 98 percent of the students walked across the bridge daily or weekly and many were already here and would be labeled "Illegal" by those who fail to understand that human beings cannot be illegal; by definition, behavior can be illegal, people cannot.

They had an open position for a teacher willing to work with juniors and seniors teaching them what they needed to know to gain some sort of legal pathway into the United States. The students oath age of 15 were considered adults in their homeland; many already had a child being tended to by their Abuela while the momma attended high school classes. Very, very few spoke or read passable English when they arrived. Fewer understood it at all. They came looking for a future not for only themselves, but for everyone in their extended family and beyond. They carried far more than backpacks on their youthful shoulders. They carried generations of a hard working people on their backs, along with the promise of hope for literally hundreds of relatives should they achieve the near impossible and earn a high school diploma in the US.

One interview and I was in. I had a great classroom on the ground floor near both the bathroom and the back door. When I arrived, I did what I always did at any new post: made friends with the main office lady by making her a lovely apple crumble and delivering a six-pack of the best local beer to the head custodian. The gifts weren't just grease for the metaphoric wheel remember, they were physical testaments that I saw them, acknowledged their power, and they had my respect. I was serving them; in hopes they would help me serve the students with whatever may be needed.

And then, that attended to, I began to do what was necessary to make myself and hopefully the students more comfortable while learning. I ditched all the desks into the hallway, including whatever gross metal and plastic thing they were calling a teacher desk and chair, and started looking around in the old storage buildings for possible replacements. Bingo. I discovered a building on campus harboring all the old science rooms' oak science lab tables and their accompanying stools. Too heavy for one person sans hydraulic lift, I sought out help. When the custodians found out what

I was up to, they were immediately all in on the project. It was unusual for anyone in the custodial or cafeteria staff to speak English. They were primarily from Mexico and journeyed with the students across the bridge daily to punch in and make a salary far better than anything they could manage on the Mexico side of the border. (Note: For those unaware of the economic nuances of such an arrangement – they pay all the usual US payroll deductions without ever hoping to collect on it. Migrant workers, despite the usual ignorance of Americans who think they're taking from a pot that isn't theirs', in actuality, according to 2008 data, each migrant actually saves taxpayers over $20,000 a year. They pay into everything and get nada. No social security, no social services, no medical assistance. Nada.)

These folks were truly support staff. Most would do anything to help in the effort to get their younger countrymen and women to achieve enough academic success that they could earn a spot in an American college or university, or even a good position in a US based corporation. They weren't only trying to get into the US just to get out of Mexico; they were trying to get their entire family out of a poverty few in the US have lived and even fewer have witnessed.

"Mira, Maestra!" they would appear at the classroom door with an overstuffed chair or loveseat, a standing lamp, a shelf. "Mira!!!"

"Mucho gusto" I would admit, then "ahhh, excelente!!! Gracias, gracias!" doing what I could to help unload the treasure into the little reading corner being created piece by piece.

I also went with a friend's truck over to inspect the big dumpsters outside a university building which was being remodeled. Round coffee table, another cozy chair, a tall bookcase, another lamp. A great rug with no stains. And we had it. A few plants and the reading corner was complete.

I found rolls of old white paper somewhere and used it with blue paint tape to cover the science tables so that the students could doodle as they learned or draw project schemes with other students; each table had a couple of containers full of markers and pens.

I was not an ESL teacher; I had no training or experience or certifications in ESL. But I had not been hired to teach ESL, and although most of the students also qualified for ESL classes and worked steadfastly to learn the basics, they also had to meet the requirements fully to graduate, and so they also needed to take their regular junior and senior English classes concurrently. Not all the students needed ESL classes; students who had been in the country longer, or had an older sibling at home who had already taught them passable English were shuffled into a couple of very small AP English classes so that the school could maintain their AP curriculum and so that students with prowess in the study of English would have the opportunity to reach for higher academic realms.

Regardless of what classes they had been relegated to in order to meet requirements, the students I was graced with on the border worked more assiduously and consistently to learn than any students I ever have worked with anywhere else before or since. Often, they did so while also working another job to earn their bed and bread each day, to contribute to the constant family effort to get the ends to meet up. I had students who went home to take over the counter of a family business for the next few hours, students who stayed with a tia or abuela during the week so they could catch a nap after school and before their night shift at one of the nearby refineries, students who cared for elderly relatives unwaveringly.

In Mexico and in many Mexican American families, once children reach age 15, they are considered adults. The young women who came from families with any means celebrate this rite of passage with a Quincineara, which as far as I can tell is a mini wedding with a bunch of groomsmen, a dramatic representation of and rehearsal for when the father walks his daughter down the aisle, which can now happen at any time, given they're all adults now, replete with adult responsibilities and expectations. And yes, marriage is expected. Procreation is anticipated within a year. Education is not a primary responsibility; it is a necessity for children so they can learn enough to get a job and contribute to the family and society. However, if a young person showed both an interest in and ability for academic work, it would likely be supported enthusuiastically such that the entire family's situation could improve significantly. However, even if a person opted for a secondary education, as adults they needed to work for money and contribute to the family as well. To contribute. To play their economical part. To be accepted into school in the US and to make the effort to get there every day and to do the work necessary to earn a high school diploma in the US wasn't enough. It was extra, a gift, a chance, not cart blanche.

One semester and I was also mentoring the new teachers in the English department. One year and I was faculty chair. And I was, as you recall, on the edge of sanity myself. I was now walking the a razor's edge I had not experienced in my decades of life as an edge walker. It wasn't as though they had teachers in the area, let alone from other places, banging down the door at human resources for a position there. You had to be crazy to walk into such a place as a teacher. I certainly fit that part of the job description. And oh how I loved a sinking ship. Loved to climb the mast and call out to everyone on and off the boat that anything is possible as I myself was gasping for breath so badly that eventually, about halfway into the second year of my time there, I had to take a medical leave of absence. And then I had to take another one.

This internal battle echoed the external one and vice versa. Despite many students doing well on the state exams the previous year, and this, despite that they were held back with exams the same way the black students had been in North Carolina for exams are not designed for most human beings in a non white culture; they are made for overweight US kiddos with parents and houses with televisions and books and magazines and they use a language not only unavailable to some demographics, but untranslatable. It may as well have been gibberish.

I do not spend much time on test prep, though I do pack a great deal into the three weeks prior to a major exam, working with students to familiarize them with the upcoming exam and teach a few basic test taking skills/cues, as well as have students remind themselves of their strengths and bolster any weaknesses. It was during one of these prep sessions that this language dilemma arose one day in a tenth-grade class one morning.

We were going over a practice exam as a class out loud so I could hear weaknesses as a group and address them before the actual exam; it also allowed students to practice taking a formal exam which is its own particular animal with its own little tricks to confuse students and test the strength of their knowledge. Seeing past the questions into and through the minds and techniques of the test makers, seeing through their insidious tricks, affords students a great deal of self-confidence, particularly for those who suffer from test anxiety – which is pretty much everyone. It also allows them to witness for themselves their strengths and weaknesses; speaking aloud in a group of trusted colleagues carries a sort of exponential strength within it that creates the potential for insights unavailable when reading silently to one's self. Additionally, this class discussion method of test review, going through a practice exam orally with the class, affords students a cumulative knowledge, allowing them to study together more efficiently and successfully; everyone learns from everyone else, hearing the actual process of is learning and struggling academically. Reading through the questions and possible answers, I read a specific question and one of the choices was "d. lawn". D was the correct answer but no one got it correct in the first round. We came back to it for a closer look.

"Okay," I took a deep breath. "Let's do this again together slowly to see what's going on here." I had a student reread the question and then we went through the answers one by one. We got to the correct response and someone read aloud, "d. lawn."

It was followed by stillness and quiet – not the usual state of this class of 28 hungry learners. And then, one of the braver voices spoke up, "What's a lawn, ms?"

All eyes moved from the courageous questioner to me. Now I was as still and quiet as they were. Ask me to define hyperbole or parallel structure or even ganglia, but such a simple word I had known since childhood? How can I explain a lawn to folks who had no experience of anything other than a dirt or gravel yard? I let the students see that I was having a tough time with this one, that they had stumped me, and I was floundering for an example they could relate to. They waited in respectful silence. Then I saw it.

"Hey," I jumped off my usual class discussion perch, the top of the teacher desk, and landed squarely on my feet. "I know where you can see a lawn!" I had their complete attention so I went with it, pointing west with my arm westerly. "You know where all the drug lords live up on the mountain?"

Now they were excited by their own knowledge. They had known all along! A chorus of excited responses pummeled me. For the most part, students from Mexico have not been enculturated to curb their enthusiasm in the name of coolness.. Stupidity and ignorance aren't so cool there, if at all. Cool was knowing where you were going and going there, challenging barriers at least daily for the sake of an education, and then working to continue family financial responsibilities – that's cool. And for guys, such things were also "chick magnet" material. It was akin to the male birds of paradise's mating performances.

More than two dozen responses in quick succession, overlapping, "Yeah, ms!" "Sure ms!" "Yes ms!" "Oh yeah!" were launched at me as I went to the board and made a skeletal bird's eye view showing a massive casa, an open space around it dotted with little balloon trees, a wall around the open space with a sidewalk between the front wall and the road. I put green exes all through the open space.

I pointed to the exed area. "You see this area between the mansion and the wall?" I asked. Nods all around, 'This, dear people" I allowed, "this is a lawn."

Lights on everywhere, eyes shining excitedly, faces wide open; their understanding both visible and audible. "Ahhhhhhhhhhhhhhhhhhh" "Cool" "Oh my tio's always trying to grown that stuff in his yard." Some nervous laughter.

"Exactly," I nabbed the cue from the student quickly. "A yard with grass is a lawn; that's exactly right!" the student who had helped beamed. One of his buddies clapped him on the back. "You go!" he celebrated along.

Unfortunately, despite our scores being the highest in the school, the school's cumulative scores hadn't accrued enough points to ward off the designation of a "priority" school. Priority schools are those which have essentially been handed over to the state education department by the feds who then hire any worker bees in education who had sold them their ideas regarding education. These worker bees do no work other than prowl hallways and classrooms to harass teachers and students into using some strange schemes to teach so that the test scores go up. These worker bees who do no work do make plenty of useless, extra, nonsensical work for the teachers and students however. They take over the principal's office as well as add many an unnecessary administrative body as well. So now these people, most of whom had no teaching experience of their own, just a plentiful array of ideas. So they moved into our school and took over, running about forcing some idiot memorization by rote learning shit that I wasn't going near. It was all about teaching to the test and the techniques and methods offered could well have come from Mars.

Or so they thought. They did take over the principal's office and he retired shortly thereafter. They were here to teach us all how to "boost" our test scores. I stopped going to faculty meetings and suggested my colleagues do the same. I told them very clearly not to bother me or my classes, using student test scores from last year to firm up my statement. I also allowed that I did not believe in their ideas hatched for money rather than for the students' learning, and that I wasn't doing anything they suggested unless it would be of immediate and remarkable value to my students. There wasn't a fresh perspective among these people. Nor a sensible one. Very few of these "consultants" had any actual classroom experience and I made for a fair momma bear when folks wanna hurt kids. Even if the kids think they are adults already.

They did make the mistake of barging into one of my classes at one point with their little white boards and markers. Their one and only intention was to increase the student scores. They weren't at all interested in real learning. Their method? Teach to the test all year. Uh, naaah. I don't think so. Though I yielded to them initially, trying to model respect for the disrespectful for my students. We were quiet and I gave them a few minutes and suggested to the students that if they offered anything that they felt would be useful for them to please grab it. I wasn't grabbing at anything but the time being wasted by these egoists and farces. After they had wasted ten minutes of our class time, I dismissed them, respectfully but firmly. I allowed that we had some vital work to continue in our minimal time together as a class and though I appreciated their efforts, we were all good here and perhaps they could focus instead on the teachers who were not actively engaged in teaching? There were plenty of them available and I was sure the students in their classes would be happy to use up their meaningless worksheets listening to some strange white people who spoke of highlighter markers and the importance of constantly retaking the practice exams in a strange, clipped English. I was not interested, nor were my students particularly. They were waiting for us to continue reading **Bless Me, Ultima** as a class, discussing it as we went. Responding in their reading journals before they pulled their belongings together to race to whatever may be next for them. They were more interested in learning for real. So was I.

We launched back into our reading aloud with each other before the door had completely closed behind our guests. When they returned a few weeks later, they asked if they could simply observe the class. I always welcomed folks who wanted to see what the students were up to and creating as long as they understood that though they were allowed to ask questions, their opinions were not needed. I also set a parameter for them that they were welcome to take notes but not to record, and that their questions would need to wait until the end of the class, when I would leave a few minutes for them to ask questions as well as for the students' questions for them. Some shifted about at this. I could have cared less about their discomfort. As far as I could tell, they all could have used a good dose of discomfort if they were ever gonna wake up to anything.

I pointed out some open seats in the back of the room and asked them to please be as quiet as possible. I also reminded them that since they were present, nothing would necessarily be what occurred in a class where we weren't under their microscope.

And so once again I came up against what was becoming a more and more common theme in public education and throughout our cultureless society. Folks with extra letters after their names, more often than not with no classroom experience, coming in to tell the teachers and students what they "should" be doing. Of course, it was yet another example of a much larger, societal configuration which I irreverently referred to earlier in this book as "the missionary position."

Standard procedure in our society is to have a bunch of fancy Nancies with little to no experience in the field who are hired for administrative positions and as consultants; they sit about their fancy tables together or at their fancy desks in a quiet office, creating policy and presenting practices which have absolutely no connection to the folks in the field, other than making more unnecessary paper or computer work for them which pulls them ever further away from their primary role – the children. This common dynamic runs through all our systems at this point in the US. It's everywhere – from convenience stores to congress – so it is logical that it is also found in our schools. I refer to it as the missionary position primarily due to the core belief and central idea from which it derives still held fast to as precious by far too many at this late date. It is the belief that can be summarized in many ways, though the most common I have witnessed are related. "I know what you need" and the related idea, merely a more specific outshoot: "In order for you to be okay/human/legal/ okay/etc, you need what has (allegedly) allowed me to be okay/human/legal/etc". Neither of these ideas are born of any real experience in the field or even any real honest discussions with the folks they aim to serve about what they see is needed; in US public schools, there is little to no student input whatsoever, though they do make efforts to pretend the students' input will be considered, it is very very rare.

Must be a close cousin of "the Peter Principle"; if you mention the dynamic to any worker anywhere in the US in any field, they shake their heads sadly or nod with eyes closed in agreement. For they are the frontline workers, the working poor, the ones who are making minimum wage and scraping by while the CEOs of their corporations vacation anywhere and anytime they wish, and they have been left to explain and even defend the latest nonsensical policy or practice to the clients or students or customers when they themselves know it is nothing but stupid. It's no different in the classroom. I failed to defend; I led revolts instead. Class by class, student by student, parent by parent, I reminded them of their individuality, their individual preciousness, their responsibility to use everything life offered as a learning opportunity.

I worked against student sublimation every chance I got. Some of the methods came in the simple form of responses to student behavior. For example, I did not yell or even raise my voice in order to get the class's attention; I only raised my voice if I was reading a story and a character's dialogue demanded it. As a matter of fact, what I had learned from students over the years was that yelling was met with deafness; the more their folks and teachers and others yelled at them, the less they listened. And why would they? It was all the same old same old anyway. While I was still with the academy, a wise old friend, in response to a parent's complaint that their child simply didn't listen despite them repeatedly telling them the same thing, suggested that rather than saying the same thing over and over, they say it for the first time, and then for the first time, and then for the first time, ad infinitum, ad nauseum. Essentially, be present; keep it always fresh. Every time. Rang true to me. The message mattered little if the attitude, and therefore delivery, was off.

Students had gone further over the years, teaching me clearly, freshly each time, that if my reaction was based on my discomfort, it mattered little to them; however, should my response originate in genuine concern for them, immediate connection and communication, and therefore understanding. However, a class full of public school students demanded further methodology and practices.

If I was called away from a classroom full of newer students for any period of time, I would re-enter to chaos, which is to say, other than one or two of the most studious people, despite the fact that these were young adults of 16 through 19, they had succumbed to their lowest form of behavior, which I chock up as "herd behavior", a more than common behavior exhibited throughout classrooms everywhere in the nation. Though not all classes need wait for the teacher person to leave the room; they were able to continue mindlessly while the teacher would scream at them just as mindlessly.

These teachers either don't last long and recall their year or years of teaching as one would a stint in the army during a war in which they served in active duty, or they stay, become bitter and mean, and often have what is referred to in school faculty rooms as well as many other places in our world as "a breakdown". I would argue that they had broken long before they ever began teaching and never did whatever work was necessary to heal their wounds. That was most certainly what happened with me; there was only so long one can get away with helping others with their own healing if one has not addressed their own goblins within. Eventually, one's own insidious incorrect ideas about one's self or others or the world will initially stifle and ultimately silence any efforts to help others. Educators, arguably one of the most essential roles played in our society other than parents, and sometimes moreso when a parent is nonexistent or less than adequate, must do everything necessary to become aware of our own circling beneath the surface ideas about absolutely everything. Our cultivated opinions, biases, prejudices, pre-conceived notions, and so many other notions often born of we not where or when, must stop being protected and defended and passed on to our next generation. If anything is to ever change in our educational system, we as teachers (and counselors, social workers, etc) must find a way to do our own work to address and resolve such notions as they arise and as we develop more of an awareness of them as we proceed. It is not a task; it is a way of life.

So the usual would occur. I would step out of the room and upon my return, bedlam. I would stand for a while in silence, yoga tree pose, in the doorway. Blank or quizzical expression on my face. One by several, the students would notice me, nudge each other, turn toward me, quiet them-selves. Wait. My repertoire had been refined somewhat from practice myself.

"Okay," I stepped further into the room and continued while I still had their complete attention. My revolutionary scholar from first period who never made it there on time but always brought along whatever his Abuela had made for his breakfast and shared it with his classmates and myself. He was at my desk, doing out his Abuela's sweet bread with his fellow students. I stopped in the middle of the room and he came over and stood next to me, offering himself as an ally. I told him I was fine and he was welcome to have a seat. He did so. Then I looked out at the still waiting faces. "Listen carefully to me now because if you hear this everything could be different for you in the future and if you don't, it could well be the same old same old." I had them.

"Whatever we practice we get good at. So if you practice needing to be told what to do, then that is what you will excel at. If you practice instead taking responsibility for your education and acting accordingly, with only yourself watching, anything is possible for you. Now, whatever you do, don't believe me. Test it this week – look around in your classes, watch your own choices and behaviors when you are on your own. See what you think."

"Damn Ms.," my budding scholar whistled, "Now yer gettin' all deep and shit on us."

I didn't need to respond; not that I would have anyway. Someone else in class said it for me I suppose. Or for some part of myself.

"She's always like this Jesus, you just don't get here enough."

It was this young man who came to me at year's end and offered me his beloved biography of **Che'**. Though he was a brilliant young man and his family wanted him to attend any of the universities to which he had been accepted on full scholarship, he decided instead to put his US education on hold and return to his ancestral homeland of Peru to learn his original language and see what happened next. I held the book to my heart and thanked him heartily. With gratitude becoming tears in his eyes,, "Hey ms?" he said, wiping his eyes with the back of one hand.

"Yes?" I asked, unsuspecting. Then he reached out and bear hugged me. "Thanks Ms. Thanks for not being just another fuckin' brick in the wall."

I smiled, inside and out. I hugged him back like the momma bear I am.

It was all I had lived for.

AFTERWORD

The core problem with schools throughout the country may well be the lack of any real education of the educators themselves, especially regarding awareness, mindfulness, selflessness, community mindedness, and many other essential human aspects. Few of us have any practices or knowledge of them that would feed both us and our students. These must be created or we will remain lost. And no, one yoga class in an SEL series for teachers ain't enough.

How on earth can they be expected to convey these qualities to the next generation? What happens to a civilization that loses the vital knowledge and practices that allow us to remember who we are and what we are doing here? That forfeits presence for pedantic? That celebrates the lowest forms of human behavior by spreading them about via social media? Can such a strand ever be caught again? Can it ever be rewoven into life's daily fabric?

Oh sure, we have all the new SEL curriculum for both teachers and students now and this is not a step in the wrong direction, simply a step that can only be taken so far within the context of the current systems. And yes, there is the newest rage, "community schools", some of which may well be of great service to the children and families they serve, though this was certainly not my experience when I taught most recently in the local southern New Mexico system. It was my experience that it was being used as yet another replay of tweaking a system here or there and naming it something catchy. I did communicate quite clearly to the school superintendent, mayor, and then "director" of community schools that they did not have anything close to resembling a community school. Then I had to wonder if the phrase was itself oxymoronic. Our nation's current schools were not created to educate, but indoctrinate. It did not evolve, as some may imagine, from the one-room schoolhouse model. It is, in fact, a model based on the assembly lines. Teachers who are working to educate are swimming hard against the current everywhere; for them, our children are not simply cans of soup or cars. Nor were they born to become more bricks in a wall.

Several years ago some of us from the academy experience took a journey into the Mexican mountain heartlands to visit with the people there; to work alongside the folks, sing songs. and share stories and meals together. At one point, Dona Sofia, our host and guide extraordinaire, village matriarch and curandara, walked us up into the hills where she had farmed and lived when she was younger. Weary from the hike and lazied by the early afternoon sun, the students sat and wrote and drew in their journals, and, one by one, fell asleep and napped on the sun-scorched hillside.

I opted instead to stay close to Sofia; I wanted to learn everything I could from her. She led me about searching for tiny old brown pods and snippets of greens. It was January, and though the flowers were blooming down in the village, here the hillside was a brown memory of a maize field and all was silent and wasted. Or so it seemed to me. At first, I couldn't see any signs of food or life. But slowly, just walking about perusing alongside Sofia, I began to discover the signs myself. I began to absorb her vision, expanding my own limited realm. By the time the others had wakened from their Sunday afternoon siesta, Sofia and I had our canvas bags full of potential food.

Later that day, the children pulled the hard-packed beans from the seemingly dead pods while Sofia prepared and steamed up the greens. As dusk made its way to the outdoor kitchen, we lit the candles and all had plenty to eat.

Teaching is like this for me. I wander along, sharing my capacities to see, to gather, to stay awake when others sleep, to walk through what may appear useless and hone perceptions, to stumble time and again and miss an opportunity; I share this entire process with the students who are most interested in staying awake themselves and finding their own possibilities and stories. And then we circle up at nightfall or early in the day when all is still and celebratory, and share with each other what we have discovered. Feed each other with the harvest. This is the most ancient and true model of teaching to me. And it is available to us all, without schools, walls, titles, degrees. If only we each and all accepted responsibility for our own education as well as that of all our children. It does indeed require a village. Everything requires a village. And yet, we have for the most part destroyed our villages, that way of life. Can we rebuild it in a way that would be more true?

I have been teaching for decades now. Sometimes in formal public school settings, sometimes to young writers in their early twenties who were hoping to become noteworthy journalists, sometimes to teenage people whom many others had given up on, sometimes to enthusiastic home-schooled children whose ideas and images lit even the dimmest of winter rooms, sometimes to elderly people who attended my little writing circles in hopes of sharing some of their life-store of knowledge and experience. I am honored to have walked in some way with each and everyone of them. To have shared enough of my own journey with them that they felt safe enough to begin to discover their own voices, and their own stories, their own way - through torments and yearnings and graces. I hope I can always be engaged in this most human of activities – learning and growing and developing and sharing life's journey in a circle of trusted others. It is a true gift and one for which I am eternally grateful.

If I had to lay claim to or propose a method or position regarding teaching, I would be hard-pressed to say more than this: share your own integral search for identity, for humanity, humility, purpose, and in particular, your own journey through life and what you have witnessed, and in so doing, offer our children the necessary tools for their own searches and needs for expression. From this, then, the teacher must create a space for others (students) that provides the safety and discipline necessary in which they may begin to develop their own tools for expression within the search for themselves. This second "step" is critical and must really accompany the first, lest the classroom become an unwilling audience for the teacher's ego. One must become a momma bear and hold fast to the purpose.

While backpacking through the Adirondacks one particularly rainy springtime, one of my students, MeeKay, and I spent what seemed hours blowing intensely and directly into a tiny flame that had finally caught on a small piece of birch bark he had climbed a tree to harvest. It was raining all about us; it had been pouring down literally for days prior to this as we hiked in the high peaks region. All the other students slept in their tents or meandered about trying to stay warm through activity, intermittently stopping by and watching intently and hopefully while Mee and I stayed true to our task. We were fueled only by Mee's "vague perception" that became less vague as we worked. The idea and images of warmth, dryness, and the camaraderie of a group that forms around a fire in even the best of weather but most certainly after hiking in the rain for a week - all of these became more real as we worked. Before long, we had a circle of warmth and song in which to feast.

The analogy relates does it not? A spark – a single ignition. And within and all around it is that notion of possibility… the effort demanded – the unceasing focused work – such that the spark might materialize into the actualization of perception – a fire that warms and gathers a circle of friends, the food gathered despite a seemingly barren hillside – and a meal prepared that feeds many. How is this any different from teaching? From learning? From being a learner amidst a community of learners? Why must we create and subvert our most amazing possibilities as a society by relegating our children and our selves to a system? To the confines of a classroom and a school? It is not only unnecessary and costly in every respect, it has become obviously ineffective and insane.